The Research Interview

Bill Gillham

continuum
LONDON • NEW YORK

Continuum

The Tower Building
11 York Road
London SE1 7NX

15 East 26th Street
New York
NY 10010

First published 2000
Reprinted 2003, 2004

British Library Cataloguing-in-Publication Data
A catalogue record for this book is available from the British Library.

ISBN 0-8264-4797-X

Typeset by Paston PrePress Ltd, Beccles, Suffolk
Printed and bound by CPI Antony Rowe, Eastbourne

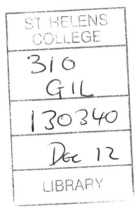

Contents

Series Editor's Foreword		vii
Acknowledgements		viii
1	The Nature of the Interview	1
2	Interviewing: For and Against	9
3	Focusing on the Interview Questions	19
4	The Interviewer as the Research Instrument	25
5	Organizing and Managing the Interview	37
6	The Use of Prompts and Probes	45
7	Piloting and Running the Interview	53
8	Carrying out a Content Analysis	59
9	Writing up Interview Data	73
10	Special Interviewing Techniques	81
Endnote: The Limits of Interview Data		91
Index		95

Series Editor's Foreword

The books in this series are intended for those doing small-scale research in 'real life' settings. No previous knowledge of research methods is assumed and the series is particularly suited to practitioners studying for a higher degree or who want to research some aspect of their practice. The thinking underlying the series reflects a major shift in social science research methods over the past fifteen years away from a natural sciences style which emphasizes deductive theory testing, a prior determination of method (usually experimental) and 'generalizable' results, towards a recognition that such requirements are often unworkable and inappropriate in the real world.

This is not a defect, because the traditionally scientific methods are often not adequate as a way of understanding how people behave 'in context'. This does not mean that one should give up an empirical, evidence-based tradition, but adapt to what is possible and, more importantly, what is likely to yield a truer picture.

Bill Gillham

Acknowledgements

The contents of this book reflect the author's experience as a practitioner-researcher psychologist, and the debts here are too numerous to list. Training practitioner psychologists has been a particular forum for getting the multitudinous details of technique into focus; more recently this has been extended to the training of research students in art and design.

At a conceptual level the author has found O. Hargie, C. Saunders and D. Dickson's 1987 book *Social Skills in Interpersonal Communication* (Croom Helm) of particular value and enduring influence. This book is strongly recommended as further reading because it is, essentially, *complementary* to the emphasis in the present volume.

Mrs Jane Cuthill battled with a virus-infected computer to produce a clean manuscript. My wife Judith cleaned it up from the point of view of style and expression. Such defects as remain represent the limitations of the author.

1

The Nature of the Interview

An interview is a conversation, usually between two people. But it is a conversation where one person - the interviewer - is seeking responses for a particular purpose from the other person: the interviewee. This may or may not be for the particular benefit of the person being interviewed. In the case of a doctor taking a medical history from a patient or a therapist working with someone who is psychologically distressed, it clearly is. In the case of a market researcher seeking information which will help in the launching of a new product, it clearly is not.

But whatever the purpose, and no matter how sensitive or person-centred the interview may be, the relationship is essentially a controlling one. 'Control' is a word with negative connotations in our day. But control in the sense of *management* is fundamental to skilled interviewing. Even so-called 'non-directive' interviewing constructs a direction from the material brought up by the person being interviewed.

The form and style of an interview is determined by its purpose. We can see this more clearly if we list a few different kinds of interview; and what they are for.

1. *Medical:* to obtain a case history so that a patient's condition can be correctly diagnosed and appropriate treatment prescribed.

2. *Selection:* to obtain information to supplement material on the CV and application form so that someone can be suitably employed.
3. *Therapeutic:* to enable the client to develop a perception of his or her difficulties which leads to insight and changed behaviour.
4. *Market research:* to obtain information so that the development and marketing of a product or service can be improved.
5. *Research:* to obtain information and understanding of issues relevant to the general aims and specific questions of a research project.

If interviews differ in their purposes they none the less have a great deal in common. The main dimension of difference is in the extent to which the interview is *structured*, and the degree to which the interviewee is allowed to 'lead' the content of the interview. Table 1.1 (reproduced in other volumes in this series) shows the structured–unstructured dimension in summary format (see p. 6).

The most structured forms of interview (common in market research) are those where the interviewer *knows* what he or she wants to find out and the interviewee just has to answer the direct questions. Precise buying habits, preferences and opinions may be unknown, but the interviewer knows exactly what *kinds* of answers are needed: in the end he or she needs to be able to put a number to these (61 per cent or whatever buy this, prefer that, think the other). Specification is achieved but no unexpected discoveries: a high degree of structure largely excludes them.

But in the same way that taking a medical history or engaging in a therapeutic interview may turn up something unexpected or go in a surprising direction, so may a research interview lead to genuine discoveries.

Research is about creating new knowledge, and the open-minded researcher cannot always be sure what direction that will take. Researchers who 'know' what they want to find out are like the doctors who 'know' what a patient's problem is: they may well be right. But they may equally well miss something. The doctor who only half listens to patients, and doesn't draw them out, may fail to register a history of symptoms that doesn't fit the familiar pattern of common ailments. It is easily done.

Pre-conceived notions are as much a danger in the research interview as in a medical interview. A kind of expert openness is the key skill in both.

Structure and flexibility

In a sense the structured–unstructured dimension is false. Expert interviewers always have a structure, which they use flexibly according to what emerges.

In a medical or therapeutic interview, the interviewer might start with a simple 'open' introduction. 'Tell me what the problem is' or 'What is it you're concerned about?' The answer could take any form and the interviewer has to have ready a structuring response to that: questioning it into shape, giving it direction.

It is this that the novice interviewer finds difficult: where do I go from here? Interviewers in training tend to feel anxious and so tend to be over-controlling – not attending to the interviewee, working relentlessly from a list of questions in their head. The interviewee will quickly find this a discouraging experience and the interview will stall.

It takes confidence to be a listener, to decentre from oneself and focus on the person being interviewed. It is *he or she* who has something to tell you: you may know your broad aim, the particular topic that you want information on, but it is only the interviewee who can provide this.

Interviewing is more than technique and one can have the experience of being put through a well rehearsed format, yet be aware that the interviewer has not drawn out the issues that really matter.

In a sense you have to learn technique and then forget about it. A footballer who practises and practises ball control at speed will react flexibly in the heat of the game, but with practised technique operating unconsciously at the back of it.

So in interviewing you start off with a question, the opening shot; where it goes from there may be unpredictable but you have to follow, controlling the direction. In a phrase, you have to keep your eye on the ball.

Skill, in any medium, is characterized by certainty and a quality of 'naturalness'. And that is really what you *are* being – responding naturally to the person you are interviewing, who will sense your interest and concern. The fact that you are technically practised doesn't detract from the dimension of naturalness. Nor does the fact that you are being deliberate and purposive.

In a research interview you are the research instrument, and you are not a standard product. Interviewing style, like writing style, is to some extent a personal business. No matter how much you learn about interviewing, it is your own personal resources which breathe life into the technique and, in a way, take over from it.

You don't just imitate someone else you have seen interviewing in a way that impressed you. You will pick up clues and bits which you can incorporate, but they will be the elements that fit *you*.

The reason for having this exhortation at the beginning of the book is that we shall be concentrating on the specifics of interviewing; and it is easy to give the impression that that is all there is to it. Nothing could be further from the truth.

Do you need to be 'interviewing' at all?

Organized 'interviews', no matter how loosely structured, have a formal quality that can make them unsuitable in some contexts. Furthermore, for some groups the word 'interview' has negative connotations (job applications; benefit claims; police questioning).

Of course, you don't have to call an interview an 'interview' - you could call it a 'discussion' or a 'chat about what I'm interested in' or whatever phrase seems appropriate. But it is important not to be dishonest - not least because some individuals will be well aware that authority figures of one kind or another regularly use such euphemisms, with some other, concealed, purpose behind them.

If you look at Table 1.1 you will see that using naturally occurring conversation is at the 'unstructured' extreme. Sometimes this is all that is possible. However, your approach will still be *organized*.

Chapter 3 describes how you focus in on your research questions and, from them, decide what *specific* questions can only be answered by talking to people. In real world research you have to use the methods that are *possible*. If you feel that the people you are involved with in your project are not sophisticated enough, or would be defensive about an organized interview, you can still ask them systematic questions – perhaps only one or two at a time as the opportunity occurs.

There is nothing dishonest about this because you will have made clear that you are a researcher trying to find answers; in a sense they will *expect* you to ask questions. You won't be able to *record* the answers, as you can in a specially set up interview, but you should write them down *as soon as possible* afterwards - just as you might write down things you have heard as part of being a 'participant observer'.

Over time you can cover a number of question topics and

Table 1.1 The verbal data dimension

Unstructured ➤ ➤ Structured

Listening to other people's conversation: a kind of verbal observation	Using 'natural' conversation to ask research questions	'Open-ended' interviews; just a few key open questions, e.g. 'elite interviewing'	Semi-structured interviews, i.e. open and closed questions	Recording schedules: in effect, verbally administered questionnaires	Semi-structured questionnaires: multiple choice and open questions	Structured questionnaires: simple, specific, closed questions

a number of people – probably more than you could comprehensively interview.

An extension of this is to invite people for 'a chat' – perhaps fifteen minutes or so – to clear up some points. Again you can keep this very informal, perhaps arranging it informally. ('Could you give me a quarter of an hour this afternoon? There are some things I'd like to ask you about.')

This will be less intensive than a full interview and you should have no material around – interview schedule, tape recorder – which would formalize things. But you will need a room where you can avoid interruption, background noise or intrusive curiosity. So this is a degree more formal, a fraction more systematic, but with a fairly loose structure so that the other person doesn't feel he or she is being 'put through their paces'.

These points, this emphasis, are being made here because the main focus of this book is on a style of interviewing which has *more* structure, although still being very 'open' in its style – what is known as 'semi-structured' interviewing. This has wide applicability and you should not assume that only 'sophisticated' people can cope with, or are comfortable with, a specially set up interview.

An interview is an interview and you don't pretend that it is anything else; you can deal with any misconceptions by explaining well beforehand, and in the process of getting agreement, what the interview is about. If you have a clear grasp of your research issues – and you certainly shouldn't attempt an interview until you have – then you will be able to communicate them simply.

An interview makes a demand on the interviewee: it signals that it is a 'special occasion'. It is impressive how people will respond to this. Quite simply you will get more out of them because they see the interview in that light. The willingness of people to work at an interview when it is of no *direct* significance to them reflects the fact that people are often not listened to; that their views and experiences are not

7

treated as being of any account. If you are interested and you *listen* you may be surprised at the richness of what emerges, expressed in a way that commands attention.

So there are bonuses in 'formality', and the setting up of an interview (see Chapter 5) can indicate very clearly how you value the contribution the interviewee is making.

A practical issue which bears on this is *where the interview takes place*. Obviously you take the convenience of the interviewee into account. Perhaps the workplace or their home is the only feasible arrangement. And there is a common assumption that people talk more freely 'on their own ground'. Sometimes that is certainly true, but those familiar contexts can also be inhibiting – quite apart from the distractions of other people.

The implied confidentiality of meeting on neutral ground can be an uninhibiting force, where the daily constraints that hedge them round are freed. If you give people the *choice*, perhaps explaining the pros and cons, then they can make the best judgement for themselves. A practical problem with meeting on *their* territory can be that recording is not possible (sound quality, background noise, etc.). But if that is where it has to take place, you have to adapt.

2

Interviewing: For and Against

Face-to-face interviews are enormously time-consuming. The actual time spent interviewing is the least of it: if no more than the hour expended on the interview was involved then you could conceivably do a hundred of them, even as a lone researcher working in your spare time. But a hundred one-hour interviews could be as much as 5,000 hours of work: you will soon see why.

The time-cost factor is emphasized because it is often grossly under-estimated, particularly by the novice researcher, the reality only dawning once you are irretrievably committed.

The extra 'cost' needs spelling out:

- *Developing and piloting the interview:* a 'shared cost' across all interviews, but still no small item.
- *Setting up and travelling to and from the interview location:* this typically involves more time than the interview itself and, of course, things can go wrong.
- *Transcribing the interview:* it is at this point that the reality starts to hit you. A one-hour interview takes about ten hours to transcribe into a tidy format: and you can't do your analysis properly unless it is written down. There *are* short cuts (described in Chapter 8) but they are not entirely satisfactory.
- *Analysing the interview:* here the time is difficult to specify

because so much to-ing and fro-ing is involved, and you will be moving from one transcript to another, categorizing the responses, and this is not a straightforward business. It is idle to suppose that a computer will do it for you, although a computer is a great help in organizing your categorical display. Another five to six hours per interview is not an over-estimate.

This 'costing' does not include the time taken in writing up your analysis.

The foregoing is not intended to discourage but to prevent you from over-committing yourself. But you may ask: wouldn't it be better to do a questionnaire? In some cases the answer is certainly 'yes', but questionnaire data are necessarily thin and don't help you to understand or explore answers. The overpoweringly positive feature of the interview is the richness and vividness of the material it turns up. In a research report using different kinds of data, the interview material is almost always the most interesting and, above all, it enables you to *see* and to understand what is reflected rather more abstractly in other kinds of data (statistical summaries, for example). It is for this reason that a *small number* of interviews is commonly included as an illustrative dimension in what would otherwise be a rather dry report that seems to have nothing to do with real people. General statements, no matter how well written, can convey less, and with less impact, than a direct quotation from an interview, even when the person being interviewed is not smoothly articulate. For example, a young single mother speaking about the breakdown of her relationship with the baby's father:

> he couldn't cope with being a father so he up and went ... I find it really difficult on my own ... because I was expecting his Dad to always be there ... he just felt

he had so much responsibility towards us ... all his money.

(From L. Burghes and M. Brown, 1995, Single Lone Mothers, p. 44)

The two factors of time-cost versus data richness balanced above are the main for and against factors. It is worth saying at this point that a general rule in research is that the easier it is to get data, the less valuable they are.

Table 2.1 summarizes the other negative and positive aspects of interviewing; below we discuss them.

Table 2.1 Is a face-to-face interview appropriate, necessary or possible?

No if	*Yes* if
Large numbers of people are involved	Small numbers of people are involved
People are widely dispersed	People are accessible
Most of the questions are 'closed', i.e predictable, factual	Most of the questions are 'open' and require an extended response with prompts and probes
A 100 per cent response is not necessary	Everyone is 'key' and you can't afford to lose any
The material is not particularly subtle or sensitive	The material is sensitive in character so that trust is involved
You want to preserve anonymity	Anonymity is not an issue, though confidentiality may be
Breadth and representativeness of data are central	Depth of meaning is central, with only some approximation to typicality
Research aims are factual and summary in character	Research aims mainly require insight and understanding

Numbers involved

Large-scale interview studies are rare because of the enormous cost involved. Even here (and perhaps especially here) various techniques are employed to cut cost. These include:

- *Telephone interviewing*, which cuts out travelling but loses the quality of face-to-face interviews. Widely used in the USA (enormous distances), it is very difficult to do well.
- *Sampling*, i.e. keeping the number of interviews to a minimum for adequate representativeness. National opinion polls on voting intentions, for example, commonly sample only about a thousand people in randomly selected areas of the country and according to a 'stratified' sample, e.g. by age, sex, occupational class.
- Severely restricting the *length* of the interview, which also usually means making it more focused.

For someone without vast resources (or when the only resource is oneself) the criterion for numbers has to be: what can I afford in terms of time-cost? That means you have to decide on the length of the interview -- which then means that you have to focus on those questions that are best answered in an interview. Practice and discipline are needed here: see the next two chapters.

Any research which aims to achieve an understanding of people in a real-world context is going to need *some* interview material, if only to provide illustration, some insight into what it is like to be a person in that setting. This can be very effective even with as few as four or five interviews of individuals carefully selected as typical, or in different positions (e.g. a couple of patients, a couple of nurses, a couple of doctors, if you are investigating the working of a hospital ward).

Accessibility

Most small-scale research is likely to be local in character, so wide dispersal is not a problem. But if, for example, you want to interview key figures in a profession, a lot of travelling might be involved. All these 'costs' have to be balanced against each other. You can strike a balance: interview a sub-sample, send postal questionnaires to others, especially those at a distance. Or you can construct a pruned set of questions and interview people over the telephone: pruned because this kind of interview is harder to keep going and the interviewee might become impatient with a long telephone call. The emphasis of this point again is that you need to be clear what you are letting yourself in for.

Balance of open and closed questions

If the questions you want to ask are straightforward, i.e. the answer is clearly indicated, adequately covered by a pre-scribed choice, then a questionnaire will suffice. And to put it the other way round, if you decide you can only afford time for a questionnaire you *have* to use almost entirely 'closed' questions (a closed question format provides a set of answers for the respondent to choose from or a rating scale). However, it should not be assumed that questionnaires are easy to construct (see the book *Developing a Questionnaire* in this series). Factual questions are best dealt with by question-naire, but anything that requires depth or exploration is not usually suitable. You *can* ask 'open' questions in a question-naire, i.e. those where the *response* is open, e.g. 'What do you think of your company's policy on promotion?' If you leave the questions 'open' the respondents have to write in what they think. However, people often can't be bothered to make an adequate response here: the task of writing being involved, and the lack of stimulus of a 'live' interview.

The other thing about 'open' questions is that people may need encouragement to say what they think and a bit of 'steering' to set them in the right direction. You may need to ask supplementary questions (*probes*) to clarify or extend the response; or remind respondents of points that they haven't mentioned (*prompts*) – see Chapter 6. Obviously these things can only be given in a live interview.

Response rate

If interviews are expensive on time, questionnaires are 'low cost', which is one main reason why they are so widely used despite their severe limitations. A major limitation is the way people respond to them (or rather, don't). We live in a questionnaire-saturated society and, unless there is some very good reason or very strong appeal, people tend not to bother.

A low response rate can be a shock to the inexperienced researcher after all, the questions are important to *you*. But if you have sent out 200 questionnaires and after a fortnight you have only had 25 back you can see that this is something you should have planned for.

There are all sorts of reasons why you *might* get a good response but, as a rule of thumb, a 30 per cent return has to be seen as fairly satisfactory, and more than 50 per cent is good. There is not the space here to go into the implications of this. In brief you need to ask 'What number *must* I get?' – and plan for the short fall accordingly.

If you can't afford to lose any of your informants then you should conduct face-to-face interviews. These could be of a highly structured format – in effect a verbally administered questionnaire (the *recording schedule* referred to earlier). But they are likely to be more useful in a semi-structured form, on the principle that if you are going to invest the time you might as well use it to the best advantage — to exploit its unique characteristics.

It is a curious fact that people are, in general, far more willing to devote an hour and a half to an interview (even of no benefit to themselves) than to give fifteen minutes to the completion of a questionnaire. There are various reasons for this, which we consider in more detail later, but a fundamental one is simple: people like the attention, they like to be listened to, they like their opinions being considered. This doesn't imply a patronizing stance on the part of the interviewer. These are human needs, which we all share, and a great strength of the interview is that, in a small way, it fulfils them.

Subtlety and sensitivity of material and the preservation of anonymity or confidentiality

You don't necessarily need to know who completed a questionnaire (although you will need to know 'subject descriptor' details like age-range, gender, occupation or whatever is relevant to your analysis). This anonymity is sometimes assumed to encourage people to disclose facts, experiences, feelings or attitudes that they would not disclose to another person. There is no good evidence in support of this assumption and, if anything, the evidence tends the other way.

If material is personally sensitive then 'letting it go', whether anonymously or not, is like letting part of yourself go. Trust and confidence are involved in making such disclosures and those are not qualities easily inspired by a questionnaire.

In any case, the issue appears to be not one of anonymity but that of confidentiality. There is a widespread resentment against even superficial personal information being held on you know not what database for you know not what reasons or uses.

Trust and confidence are interpersonal qualities – quite soon established, as experienced interviewers know. It is, in fact, remarkable what people *will* disclose if they feel you are a person they can talk to. Let us hope that that faith is not misplaced.

But apart from the issue of confidentiality – which means explaining to the interviewee the purpose of the research, how interview material is stored, analysed and interpreted and, above all, what *use* it is going to be put to – there is the fact that sensitive material is often subtle. And subtle material is not the stuff of questionnaires.

Complex human experiences are not things that people can glibly speak about in an organized fashion. A good deal of 'teasing out' is required and only skilled interviewing can do this. Much of a therapeutic interview is of this character.

Breadth versus depth

Of course, one would like to have both: a representative range of people (however the group is composed – schoolteachers, trainee police officers, junior doctors, etc.) and 'in-depth' insightful information and understanding of them as individuals. In a sense this is about the competing virtues of two 'main methods' – the *survey* and the *case study*. Surveys give you large-scale data that are relatively superficial; case studies give you in-depth data with limited claims to representativeness. The two methods are often combined (particularly illustrative case studies supplementing large-scale surveys).

Whether you go for one or the other – and in most small-scale research you have to make a choice – depends on the aim of your investigation. If you want a 'representative' picture you will probably have to use survey methods of a time-economical kind (questionnaires, the analysis of existing records), although in some instances you may interview 'representative' individuals – for example, in terms of seniority, or specialism, or whatever marks people out.

This is a key planning decision which will determine the character of your research, and it involves keeping in the forefront the central question: What do I need to know?

Factual versus insight research

This distinction overlaps with the previous one but it isn't quite the same and in conjunction will tip the balance in terms of the methods you adopt.

'Facts' are usually 'on the surface' – accessible in one form or other. Some factual data about individuals are more confidential or sensitive than others. But if the information is not sensitive then you won't *need* an interview, and to see people individually to collate straightforward information is certainly a wasteful use of time *unless* the group you are dealing with would find questionnaire completion (like form-filling) an onerous task. Incidentally, this is not a small consideration: large sections of the population are not comfortable with *any* kind of written response. And people, as a whole, find it much easier to talk than to write, even if the writing doesn't amount to much.

A strand that runs through all the dimensions discussed above is: what do you want to find out? Your research needs determine the methods you use. Methods don't come first, research questions do. You then have to ask yourself: which methods would best help me to achieve the answers to these questions?

The companion volume in this series, *Case Study Research Methods*, will help you to review the particular techniques or methods, but the present book assumes that you need to obtain in-depth data which will give you insight and understanding of particular individuals. This is an 'expensive' method, as we have emphasized before, but one with unique strengths. But because it is expensive you use it only for what is necessary, to get the data which can be obtained in no other way.

3

Focusing on the Interview Questions

Focusing is a progressive process: you start from a very wide angle, one that takes in the whole scene.

In a research project as a whole you will have a range of different research questions which will be answered in a range of different ways: by observation, by analysing records, by collecting and analysing documents, by assembling samples of things produced or made and by what people *tell* you in one way or another.

As we saw in Chapter 1, you can get people to tell you things in different ways, varying from the entirely natural – ordinary conversation (which you can use systematically) - to highly structured and 'impersonal' questionnaires. The technique you choose needs to fit the character of what you are asking. If it is relatively factual or straightforward then a questionnaire is appropriate; if it requires an elaborated 'in-depth' response then you need a semi-structured interview; if a casual, unreflected response will suffice then you should use naturally occurring opportunities in ordinary conversation.

Because both naturalistic and survey research — but particularly the former - involve a progressive clarification of the questions you want to ask, in parallel with that process you need to keep in mind the range of techniques.

Real-world research involves keeping an informal log where you record a range of material: things people have said to you, what you have observed, things to be followed up, insights or hunches – a thousand and one details that you may lose if you don't record them. Questions that you may want to ask of people are just one example of what you need to keep a note of, informally but systematically. At an early stage they may not form themselves into precise questions, but *topics* of enquiry: working conditions for nursing staff on night duty; support services for disabled college students; the value of INSET for teachers; the response to complaints by a factory workforce. As you find out more, more specific questions emerge.

The overriding consideration here is: what questions, for the purposes of the research, can only be answered by asking people? And how are those questions most efficiently posed or presented?

At some point in your preliminary investigation, not immediately but quite early on, you should start noting down questions and topics under different 'technique' headings: which ones could be dealt with in a questionnaire, and so on.

Gradually the lists will grow. As they do you will need to reorganize the groupings of them: questions that go together under one topic heading (job satisfaction, quality of teaching supervision or whatever). You will also find, as your grasp on your research project progresses, that you can *prioritize* topics you want to ask about – this is important whatever technique you use, but especially for semi-structured interviews.

Pruning the list

If you feel you can't let anything go, you are almost certainly not being rigorous enough. Shorter questionnaires are more likely to be answered than longer ones. Shorter interviews are less of a burden to analyse. You cannot include everything that might be relevant or useful; by pruning your list you are more likely to focus on those topics that your respondents will see as interesting or worthwhile. Questions also need to be distinct from each other – each dealing with a separate facet of the topic.

This is motivating for the interviewee, who will feel there is something fresh to say; but, importantly, questions that are distinct will throw up material which is distinctive in its content. This greatly eases the task of analysis. If, in the phrase beloved of politicians, there is 'clear blue water' between each question then you won't get answers that overlap the responses to *other* questions. It means that when you do your categorization you can treat each question quite separately – see Chapter 8, on *content analysis*.

The *emergent* character of 'interview' questions cannot be emphasized too strongly. The way to construct a disastrous interview or questionnaire is just to sit down and knock out a set of questions off the top of your head. As anyone with experience in higher education will testify, this is all too often how it is done by students at many levels. The resulting data are not only poor but often virtually impossible to analyse.

Because the *semi-structured* interview is a key technique in 'real-world' research, from this point on it is the development of these that we shall focus on. The use of special techniques the 'elite' interview, group interviews, telephone interviewing, recording schedules and so on is dealt with in Chapter 10. The development and use of questionnaires is a major topic in its own right and is covered in a separate volume in this series: *Developing a Questionnaire*.

For the next five chapters the word 'interview' refers only to the semi-structured variety.

Trialling your interview questions

Trialling involves trying out possible questions – usually on someone neutral, i.e. not in the setting you are researching, but preferably from the same kind of occupational or age group, whatever is relevant for purposes of simple comparison. If your project is located in a school then it isn't sensible to try out your questions on a factory worker, for example.

Trialling is distinct from *piloting*, which is an advanced stage of interview development where you give the research interview, in a developed state, in a dummy run in either the actual setting you are researching or one closely analogous to it.

Trialling questions does a number of things:

- It gives you some sort of feel for the interviewing process – a perception that it is not as simple as one might have expected.
- It alerts you to the range of factors that give an interview flavour and direction: the 'management' dimension.
- It focuses you on what it is about questions that makes them productive and stimulating – or the contrary.
- It highlights *key* questions and indicates those that are redundant, and those that need rethinking.

To an inexperienced interviewer the overwhelming impression is that there seem to be too many things to attend to at once; and that uncomfortable feeling that there are things you have missed.

In other words, it is just like the beginning stage of getting on top of any skilled activity: remember your first attempts at driving a car, when there seem to be too many knobs and switches and levers *and* you have to watch the traffic *and* use the mirrors *and* signal. Yet the experienced driver does all these things without seeming to think about it.

This brings us back to the first point: that if you are going to be a polished performer you have to make a 'hands on' start once you know more or less what you have to do, but can't yet actually do it. This mildly anxiety-making, rather uncoordinated stage is a necessary part of the process. Thinking and practice have to interact; one feeding into the other in a cyclical process of development.

In trialling the questions you simply say to your subjects: 'Look, I don't know my way around these questions yet, so apart from responding to them I'd be glad of any other comments you'd care to make -- if you feel I haven't phrased them right, or I'm focused on the wrong thing.' This example of what you *might* say is to emphasize the point that your trialling subjects can be very helpful, particularly if you are explicit about the need for feedback.

You don't try out all the questions or topics at one go -- unless they are few. If you focus on one topic area at a time then you can improve that sector and clarify it before moving on to another.

No matter how well you have thought through the topics or questions, the actual running of them will be a chastening experience. This is reality, not something you have worked out on paper or in the comfort of your own head. You are testing your 'product' and there is no substitute for it -- in any domain.

Progressive trialling

Trialling is a protracted process. The more you do the more you will see you need to do. New questions, revisions of questions, reorganization of topics, question order -- all need trying out.

You will make rapid progress in the sense that gross inadequacies -- glaring defects that are downright embarrassing will be quickly remedied. But there then comes a slower stage, but still essential, which is the process of refinement. Much of the content of succeeding chapters is addressed to this stage of interview development. Time and practice are of the essence. In particular you will become aware that there is a great deal more to interviewing than simply asking questions.

For interview development purposes this means that you

focus on elements other than the questions themselves. For example:

- ways in which you can encourage people to talk other than by asking direct questions;
- *steering* the interviewee so as to keep him or her on the topic and moving in the right direction (not least the key skill of being able to move people on so that they don't get bogged down);
- attention to the *structure* of the interview — introduction, development, closure;
- your sensitivity to what interviewees communicate non-verbally, by how they 'behave' and *paralinguistically* - by tone of voice, emphasis or emotional quality;
- attention to what is communicated to the interviewee by the setting and preparation of the interview, the 'style' you adopt, your awareness of how you come across.

This last point is the one we shall deal with first. In an interview you are uniquely the 'research instrument'. To be aware of how that instrument works you have to get to know yourself in an unfamiliar way.

4

The Interviewer as the Research Instrument

We all know ourselves, of course. Who better? Indeed. Unfortunately, and by definition, we don't know ourselves as others perceive us. We will all have had some uncomfortable experiences of this — evidence that doesn't match one's self-perception — which we will, characteristically, have tried to explain away.

The discomfort of those unflattering fragments quickly fades and, as a source of useful knowledge, they don't often amount to much. As an interviewer you need a much more comprehensive and analytic self-awareness.

Our typical knowledge of what we look like is itself severely restricted — the familiar picture in close-up, relatively immobile and expressionless, in the reverse image of a mirror tells us nothing of how we appear to another person in the social interaction of an interview. It is, in any case, far more than a matter of our physical appearance — no matter how preoccupied with that we may be. A 'good appearance' is a help in most social situations (not least when one is appearing as a defendant in a court of law) but it is not the complete answer for successful interviewing.

The use of video

Video offers the potential for changing our view of ourselves.

Its value in becoming a skilled interviewer and in practising a particular interview is at several levels.

By showing you in interaction with another person it shows you a dimension of yourself that you normally never witness. The first experience, it has to be allowed, can be something of a minor emotional trauma: if you play back the tape several times you will become more detached and analytic. Note that you should do this on your own. Watching, as part of a group, a tape of yourself interviewing is probably not useful until you have made some progress in your interviewing technique. Before that it is a socially traumatic and self-conscious experience.

Some superficial effects will appear very quickly: for example, if you find that you laugh too much or say 'um' every five words. Superficial mannerisms that are obtrusive can disappear once we are fully aware of them - sometimes without conscious effort.

However, you need to look at yourself analytically and not just impressionistically. It is useful to have a simple proforma with headings that require you to look at the *organization* or successive *stages* of the interview, and also the *skills* involved in all these stages. An example of this kind of proforma is given in Figure 4.1, but this should not be used until you have studied the later chapters   particularly those concerned with organizing and managing the interview (Chapter 5) and the use of prompts and probes (Chapter 6).

The physically static nature of an interview means that you can set up video equipment without involving anyone else; and you will soon find that you are hardly aware of its presence. Video is an invaluable part of practice. Reading this book, in itself, won't turn you into an interviewer; reading it *in tandem* with carrying out practice interviews will take you a long way even without any other kind of supervision or feedback. And that practice needs to start early, even while you are still at the question or topic try-out stage. The important point is that you take a systematic look

ORGANIZATION	SKILLS/PROCESS
Introductory stage	Non-verbal behaviour
Opening up/opening out phase	Listening/encouraging
	Questioning/Probing
Summary and closure	
	Reflecting

Note under these headings any points for your own use in skill development, or for subsequent interview development.

Figure 4.1 Interviewing: evaluation grid.

at yourself. If you are following a course it may be of value to have your supervisor sitting in; but you can do it perfectly well by yourself. For most of us that is a great deal more comfortable.

Practising interviewing

The practice phase is concerned with interviewing *skill* rather than interview *content*. That doesn't mean the content is of no consequence, but it isn't what your skill development is about. Box 4.1 contains a basic interview schedule (including prompts) which the author uses with some of his research students. In a simple way it allows them to deal with the introductory and closing phases of the interview (using their own style) and to develop awareness of and skill in developing the responses of the interviewee, especially in the difficult area of *probing*.

It may be that you don't have that kind of ready-made opportunity for practice, in which case you have to set it up for yourself. The actual question content can be made to fit the individuals and their situations: but something to do with career/professional development has enough dynamic to make it real without being so personal that you get complications that are unwanted.

Active listening

Most 'interviewers' talk too much. It is the interviewees who have the information. The worst kind of interviewer puts words in their mouths (presumably regarding them as 'inarticulate') but that way, of course, one learns nothing.

Skilled interviewers are remarkable for the economy of what they say. And through the clarity of that economy they

Box 4.1

Explain that the purpose of the research is to achieve a better 'fit' for the course to students' needs

Key questions

1. How did you come to take this course?

Prompts (if necessary)
motivation
information
research orientation

2. What were your expectations of it?

level
academic character
work load

3. What difficulties has it presented you with?

workload
organization of time
unfamiliarity of material

4. What do you think you are getting out of it?

personally
conceptually
career direction

5. What use do you think it is going to be to you?

research direction
jobs/career development
changed perceptions

Explain what you are going to do in the data analysis, e.g. content analysis and classification of main categories, informing course development.

are able to steer interviewees to reveal what they know that is relevant to the focus of the interview.

The fundamental skill is allowing and encouraging the interviewee to respond. You have to *listen*, but listening is not a passive business.

Listening: the non-verbal dimension

It would be easy to treat what follows as a set of superficial points of 'skilled' technique which, if adopted, will turn you into a socially skilful listener.

The idea that effective social interaction is just about acquiring 'social skills' is facile in the extreme: the motivation, the real feeling or interest, has to be there behind it. Indeed, when we perceive this emotional reality and honesty in someone, we can forgive or disregard an 'unskilful' expression. There is something cold-blooded and off-putting about being treated in a 'socially skilled' manner. If you are not really interested in the interview topic, and therefore in the responses of the person you are interviewing, then it won't work; in a myriad of small ways you will show that you are just going through the motions.

This doesn't mean that you ignore technique: your interest, concern, desire to learn can be impeded in various ways so that you are genuinely misunderstood. When you watch yourself on video you may see that you don't come across as you felt or intended. A few pointers will help you to focus on key aspects.

Facial expression

The face is the main communicator but our expression is often more impassive or ambiguous than we realize. This doesn't mean that one should adopt a fixed smile, undiscriminating in its character. A smile can conceal more than it reveals and it is as well to remember Somerset Maugham's observation that an unusually attractive smile often conceals an unusually nasty nature. Your facial expression has to be appropriate, and to be seen as responsive.

Eye contact

The eyes are the most communicative part of the face, as we all know from our social experience. In an interview eye contact can signal interest, expectation of an answer and much more. It is something to use sparingly – which is why, in an interview, you do not normally sit directly opposite the person you are interviewing. Too much eye contact makes people feel embarrassed or 'dominated'. Appropriate in an interrogation!

Head nods

This is something that *can* be very mechanical. Overdone it can appear frankly idiotic; subtlety and 'understatement' characterize the most effective use of non-verbal 'messages'. But used *very sparingly* it can be a powerful means of encouraging people to continue talking or to talk more fluently or confidently. The author uses this in seminars when a less confident student starts to make a contribution, rather hesitantly but, taking the cue of encouragement, quickly becoming more fluent.

Gesture

There are large individual differences in the use of gesture and we are usually unaware of our particular pattern. And there is a large *international* variation. Italians, for example, use a lot of gesture to supplement an already very expressive language. The variations and subtleties are enormous. The Gallic shrug, to take another example, can be

31

used to express a whole range of emotions — indifference, amusement, tolerance, despair. And despite national variations gesture has an international quality — exemplified in the art forms of dance or mime or clowning. In other words, this is a big topic and an under-rated one. It isn't *just* natural, it is something learned, however unconsciously.

When you watch yourself on video, one of the things you should look for is how *you* use gesture: how effective it is, or how appropriate, how you could develop its use while still feeling comfortable with it. Again, restraint and understatement seem to work best: an extended hand, palm upwards, may be a more potent invitation to respond than a direct question.

As with interviewing in general, you have to develop *your* style in this particular dimension.

Physical proximity and contact

Again there are big personal variations here. But most people feel a little uncomfortable if you get too close to them: they feel their 'personal space' is being invaded. People who are uncomfortable don't interview well. Moreover, we live in an age where there is greater awareness of the threat of physical or sexual harassment or exploitation: it is possible to give off uncomfortable, and unintentional, 'messages'. A lack of awareness here also reflects a lack of sensitivity — which communicates something in itself.

At the same time, you can 'keep your distance' too far. Most of us have an awareness of a comfortable distance — in the 'interested' but not too personal zone — perhaps four to six feet away.

Actual physical contact is even more subtly graded; but there are big individual differences. Some people don't like being touched *at all*; some people are naturally 'touchers', as a form of gesture.

It would be naive to specify what parts of someone else's body it is socially permissible to touch. If you need guidance on that you shouldn't be interviewing anyone. But it may be that you use touch too freely · watch a video of yourself again -- and are not being sufficiently sensitive to how people feel about this.

Posture and orientation

We mentioned the need to use eye contact sparingly. This is most easily 'rationed' if you are not sitting directly opposite someone: the 90 degree angle orientation makes it easier to avoid excessive eye contact. It also has a less authoritarian connotation. There should be no need to point out that, whatever angle you sit at, you should not be interviewing from behind a desk!

Posture is a particularly potent form of communication. Very simply, leaning forward, even slightly, indicates a positive attitude, or heightened interest or awareness. Leaning back indicates some kind of withdrawal – perhaps uncertainty, disagreement or boredom. But it depends on context and how it is done: it may signal reflectiveness; it is certainly a way of giving *emphasis*. Again you need to look at your 'natural' repertoire. Changes in posture may be a way of underlining what you *say* for example, suddenly sitting upright in response to what the interviewee has said, and saying: 'I think that's a very important point I hadn't thought of that.'

All these points of detail: what a complicated business they make interviewing seem! To retrieve an earlier analogy: skilled performance in football involves attention to detail: sustained analysis and practice, which is then subsumed and becomes 'natural' and unconscious.

Listening: the verbal dimension

You could tell from what he said that he hadn't listened to what I was telling him.

How often one hears complaints of that kind. How you respond verbally is a major source of encouragement (or the reverse) to the interviewee. The overriding quality is one of *alertness*, and sensitivity: you have to show in what you say and the way you say it that you have picked up the nuances and are listening hard – concentrating on *them* and not on yourself. There are two key points.

The use of voice

Whatever words you use, the tone in which you say them will convey as much as or more than what you say. The lack of conviction that characterizes so many politicians is often because one senses that they are saying the right things for the wrong reason (which Christopher Fry called 'the ultimate treason'). It isn't that the words one uses aren't important but rather that the tone cancels them out, or qualifies them.

But it may be that your voice doesn't convey the feelings of concern or interest that you *do* feel. Like a lack of facial expression, it is something you can attend to and work on without behaving in a false or unnatural way. We may *think* we sound responsive but we can't hear our own voice as others do – and this is true in the acoustic sense as well as in the sense of the familiar but inaccurate preferred perception of ourselves.

Listening rather than talking

What point is being made here? Of course when you are interviewing you will be listening rather than talking.

Unfortunately most people don't listen, in the same way that they don't observe. Everyday 'conversation' is often a kind of jostling, with the nominal listener more or less impatiently waiting for his or her turn (and often not doing that – 'overtalking' and pushing the speaker to one side, metaphorically).

Becoming a listener rather than a talker is the biggest single problem in interviewing training. Not only do novice interviewers often do most of the talking, they will sometimes scarcely leave space for interviewees to respond; and then rush on to answer for them. ('Of course, you must feel', etc.)

This is where a video recording of yourself can be very revealing. But what lies behind this apparent desire of the nominal 'interviewer' to flood the interviewee and dominate the interaction? There are a number of elements:

- *Interviewer anxiety:* a desire to make things work and to 'get a response' may make the interviewer feel that he or she has to push the thing along, to 'make it happen'. Unfortunately this usually has the reverse effect – with mounting anxiety on the interviewer's part.
- *Lack of confidence in technique:* a related issue, which manifests itself in a kind of impatience. Interviews are sometimes slow to start, with interviewees getting their bearings. It is at this stage that you have to signal that the response is up to them: you have to give them *time* and *space*.
- *A failure to appreciate the active role of silence:* you ask a question and you don't get an immediate answer. It isn't that nothing is happening, and such silences are shorter than they seem. But an interview doesn't have to go like ping-pong. *Your* silence may be equally important, indicating that you are thinking about the response that has just been made or that *you* don't have the answer to the question.

Silence has a curious potency – actors use it as a form of emphasis: of what they have just said or are about to say. It can also signal a change of direction. You don't let it go on for ever, but often all that is necessary to move things on is a simple prompt ('What do you think?' etc.) or an interrogative movement of the head.

So it is more than just cutting back on your contribution: there is technique to it. In fact, if you talk less and listen more you will be able to 'steer' the interview more effectively, in the right direction and at the right pace – because you won't be doing all the work. Not doing most of the talking signals to interviewees that that's *their* job, that *they* are the focus of the interview.

5

Organizing and Managing the Interview

The topics and questions that you are clarifying and developing have to be inserted in some overall structure. This doesn't have to be elaborate (better not) but you do need a clear idea of the framework you are using – on which the detail rests.

Initially you can think of it in terms of four main stages:

- the introductory phase;
- the opening development of the interview;
- the central core of the interview;
- bringing the interview to a close, both socially and in terms of content.

Even in a short interview the first and last of these are important, but often neglected because they are not *centrally* what the interview is all about. But attention to them helps to get the interview content into shape, and this is particularly true of the introductory phase where you explain the purpose to the interviewee. 'Closure' – bringing the interview to a close – includes an element of *reviewing* what has been covered: and important additional material may emerge even at this point.

The introductory phase

This isn't just a matter of what you say in an 'introductory' way at the beginning of the interview. It starts in advance of the actual interview.

Before they come to the interview the people concerned need to have:

- a clear idea of why *they* have been asked;
- basic information about the purpose of the interview and the research project of which it is a part;
- some idea of the probable length of the interview and that you would like to record it (explaining *why*);
- a clear idea of precisely where and when the interview will take place.

Much of this is first dealt with in person (although perhaps over the telephone), *but you confirm everything in writing.* Particular care has to be taken over the last, practical part if the meeting place is not familiar to the interviewee. You should include: a photocopied section of a street or campus map; precise instructions as to the location of the room if the building is a large one; details of how to get in touch with you if there are queries or changes or things go wrong.

This 'efficiency' aspect is partly so that valuable time isn't wasted (and possible confusion is avoided). But it is much more than that. The fact that you have taken the trouble to consult and inform people carries its own message: that you are taking the interview seriously; that you appreciate their cooperation: that the occasion is important to you; that you respect their rights and feelings in the matter. These factors (or the obverse) will have a marked effect on the attitude of interviewees, and their mental preparation for the interview.

It is the same thing with the setting and its arrangement. What messages do they convey? Are the room and the chairs you will be using reasonably comfortable? Does the room look 'organized' and prepared? Do you have refreshments to offer (the interviewee may have had to travel)? Are you prepared in all practical respects? These details are not trivial: and in combination they add to (or detract from) the 'message'.

What does your appearance convey? It is not a matter of whether you are formally dressed (though a markedly 'informal' appearance may suggest a carelessness of attitude) but if you are dressed with a bit of care that conveys something positive.

If you are going to record the interview it is necessary to make sure that you are *entirely* familiar with the machine and that *in position* it records conversation well (but you will need to check this again at the start of the interview). If you aren't prepared in this respect it is easy to get flustered: this is not impressive and it can lead to mistakes.

Make sure you are in the interview room well ahead of the appointment time. This is common courtesy, and it can be a source of confusion if you are late, another 'message' conveyed.

This pre-interview stage has been spelt out at some length because it is important and because it is often entirely missed out in books dealing with interviewing 'technique'. Technique is only half the picture.

The introduction (like 'closure') has its 'social' components: a handshake, a question about their journey, an offer of refreshment. Introduce yourself by name, but not by title (a lack of taste, which makes things appear more formal than necessary: 'I'm Janet Jones'). If the interviewee chooses to address you by your first name then that cues you to do the same; but don't assume that all people are willing to accept that from a stranger without that 'guide'.

Your manner initially should be low-key – not *too* friendly, certainly not too familiar. An undiscriminating 'friendliness' can be very off-putting because it is perceived as false. It can also be seen as insufficiently respectful – especially important when there is a big age difference. Essentially, it is a matter of thought and sensitivity.

The interview itself: opening development and substantive content

At this point we haven't started the actual interview, but in a sense it can clearly be seen that we *have*: that the tenor of the whole thing is partly determined.

Begin by explaining not just the purpose of the interview, but the purpose of the research. You will have mentioned this in your letter or on the telephone but you need to expand on that a little and also ask the interviewee if he or she has any questions about it.

Explain why you prefer to record the interview: how you will transcribe and analyse it, and deal with the issue of confidentiality. If they are comfortable about being recorded explain that you need to double-check that the machine is recording and playing back satisfactorily.

You should have your questions (and simple 'prompts' for topics the interviewee might omit to mention) on one or two sheets on a clipboard in full view in front of you. You can say, 'I've got my list of questions here to remind me. Can I start by asking you ... ?' This 'openness' will encourage the interviewee to be correspondingly open in response; if you hug your clipboard to you that conveys the sense that what is on it is something 'secret'.

A sample schedule is given on p. 29 and you can see how simple it can be. This is to your benefit: an elaborate schedule with too many questions can easily cause you to lose your way. Note that the questions in the example given, while all 'on the topic', are all distinctively different. Elaboration within them comes from how you handle the interviewee's responses, i.e. steering them but allowing them to *lead* you.

For some interviews you will need to supplement the basic factual information (which you should have obtained before the interview) – such things as the 'history' of how the interviewee has reached the present point in their professional or personal life. Such questions are 'closed', i.e. specified, by their very nature. But you need to move on from this before a 'question-and-answer' style is established, i.e. where the interviewee just answers your specific questions instead of *responding* to the topics you raise.

In a semi-structured interview the main questions are 'open' – where you are raising the topic and indicating the *kind* of answer but where the actual answers are entirely up to the interviewee.

Question *order* should display some sort of logic (chronological, thematic) so that one question could be seen as 'following on' from the previous one – which is some level of preparation for it. One of the things you will discover in your progressive question-trialling is that you are *not* getting the order right.

The other point you have to watch is that your questions are *genuinely* open, i.e. that they don't signal the desirability or the expectation of a particular answer. Tone of voice can do this, even when the words don't, e.g. the way you might say, 'What do you think of recent government legislation on this?'

If you start with a beginning question which is wide open, that sets the tone for the style of response you are expecting. For example, 'How did you first come into nursing?' One can see how that question could be a starting point for the examination of the interviewee's present feelings and attitudes about the profession – reflecting back on his or her initial expectations.

The logic of the order of substantive questions in an interview is difficult to specify because the variety of interviews is so vast – as many as its precise purposes. But later questions can take a more *prospective* form, e.g. 'What are your views on the future of the profession?'

Because interview development which means the development of the interviewee's responses – is a major topic in its own right, and not just a matter of organization, it is not dealt with here, but in the next chapter. The essential point, however, is that the interviewer's task is to ask initial questions that allow the interviewee to determine the answers, and to follow up the responses which focus the interviewee and encourage him or her to elaborate where necessary, or cover aspects of the answer that have been omitted.

Closure

Like preparation, this is an easily neglected phase of the interview. It is easy to give interviewees the impression that you have got what you wanted and just want to hurry them off the premises. Carelessness here can undo much of the previous good work, common courtesy quite apart.

There are two main elements to closure: pulling together the content (cognitive) and the more obvious 'social' element. You signal this phase in various ways so that the whole thing has a kind of shape: topics or questions that indicate that they are the 'last chapter'. And you can follow this up simply by saying 'Now the last thing I want to ask you about is . . .', or some such phrase.

Sometimes it is useful to *summarize* what you think you have learnt from the interviewee so that he or she can give you feedback on your summary impression. And this can call forth material that emerged nowhere else, occasionally of major significance (incidentally a common experience in therapeutic interviews).

And when the response has run its course, switching off the recorder indicates that the substantive phase is done. Some appreciative comment is needed here: 'You've given me a lot of useful material there – I'm very grateful' endorses the value you place on the session. If you go on to explain that you will be preparing a summary report (of the two-page variety) and/or doing a presentation – and indicate when – you can offer to send the interviewee a copy or invite him or her to the presentation. People often have the experience of contributing to research and then hearing nothing about it.

The offer you make here as part of the interview closure should be followed up by a letter that repeats the offer as well as your thanks. To some extent the impact of your research is going to depend on the observation of such courtesies – particularly if you are aiming at a primarily local effect.

So there is a little work to be done, even when the interview is over; which may take only a few minutes but which will leave either a good or a bad impression.

6

The Use of Prompts and Probes

The use of 'open' questions doesn't mean that you have no control over the way the interviewee responds. Indeed, your (unobtrusive) control is essential if you are going to achieve your research aims, i.e. you need to 'steer' for the *direction* and also ensure that *key points* or topics are covered. The first of these involves the use of 'probes'; the latter the use of 'prompts', and we will deal with these first.

Developing prompts

These go hand in hand with the development of *questions*. As you trial your questions you will be adjusting the wording, eliminating some or combining them, changing their order.

What you need to do at the same time is to note the main *points* and *topics* that your try-out subjects come up with in their answers. While each interviewee comes up with elements that are unique or peculiar to them, there will be common components that *every* interviewee needs to address: these give you your prompts (where you simply ask: *what about ...?*). Other aspects of your research (in policy documents, what you observe or overhear) will also suggest things that should go on your prompt list.

If in their response to your questions the interviewees cover those points then you obviously don't need to prompt them – but they are there to remind you. Usually there is an obviously right moment to prompt, i.e. when they have been talking about a related topic so that the prompt can seem like a natural follow-on. It is not a matter of you asking the interviewee to deal with something that he or she doesn't want to talk about, or has nothing to say on; in the flow of conversation, things get overlooked.

For your research coverage it ensures a degree of standardization – of comparability from one interviewee to another. *This is critical when you come to do your content analysis* (see Chapter 8).

Prompts are quite simple to develop and easy to use: what is described here is a sufficient guide. The use of probes is another matter – the single most difficult thing in interviewing.

The use of probes

Probes are supplementary questions or responses which you use to get interviewees to feed you more -- to expand on their response, or part of it.

The need to use a probe, and precisely what kind, depends on what the interviewee is saying. Since you can't predict what that will be, in any precise sense, you can't anticipate exactly when a probe will be necessary; and the form of it will have to 'fit' the kind of development you are seeking at that moment.

Probes – and good questions in general -- have the qualities of good writing: simple, clear, direct and potent. They need to be uncomplicated because they need to have an immediately focusing, directing effect.

There are several different kinds of probes, but it should be mentioned here – because it will be dealt with last that the most effective probe of all – *reflecting* – doesn't involve questioning at all, but simply bouncing back something the interviewee has said (or part of it) so as to get him or her to focus on and expand that element. However, we shall work through different kinds of probes, dealing with the most obvious ones first.

Clarification

If you ask people to clarify things for you you are asking them to work on what they have just said. This way they will give you more material. You shouldn't ask for clarification as a 'device' (people soon pick up this kind of dishonesty). You may have a fair idea of what they mean – but you can't be sure; and it isn't for you to decide what they are trying to say or implying.

So you say something like: 'I don't quite understand that' or 'Can you spell that out for me?' Note that the actual form of words you use should be something that is 'natural' to you and comfortable for you to use. In normal conversation we have a repertoire of set phrases which we use flexibly, and in an unconscious process of selection, to fit a particular moment.

Getting people to explain things to you is a simple but effective way to encourage them to work on their own material. Doing so often leads them to insights that they wouldn't achieve without that demand. Therapists use this approach as a main technique for helping people to achieve insight into their psychological problems: whether it *changes* anything is, of course, another matter.

But asking people to clarify for you – and this is true of most 'probing' – in a sense puts them in control: they are telling *you* and helping *you* to understand. To an important degree they are 'owning' the interview. This does not contradict the earlier point about the interviewer being in control of the interview session. The interviewer's control is of direction, and topics covered, and their order; the actual *content* is determined by the interviewee.

Showing appreciation and understanding

This may not sound like a form of 'probing' but people will expand on what they are saying if you demonstrate these qualities. This works best if it is oblique; if it is too direct it comes across as patronizing. You also have to watch your tone of voice: the overtly 'caring' or 'compassionate' note can be offputting. A straightforward comment is all that is required, but an appreciative choice of words is important, e.g. 'How did you cope with that?', 'That must have been very difficult' or 'I can't see that you had any choice.'

Justification

In an interview people often make judgemental statements – about themselves, about others, about circumstances. There may well be a lot behind this ('I'm not good at that sort of thing', 'There's no use complaining to the management', 'You just can't work effectively because of the atmosphere in this place'). You ask something like: 'What makes you say that?' Again, this should be in a form that feels natural for you, and *appropriate* to what the interviewee has just said.

Judgemental statements are summary; *understanding* them means that what lies behind them has to be unpacked and examined. Judgements are also a stop on thinking, so that asking for justification leads to an active process of *re*thinking. If you are going to get to *meaning*, the major purpose of the interview, it has to be active in this sense.

Relevance

In an interview, as in conversation in general, people can be rather elliptical – making leaps from one thing to another which are connected in their minds but slightly bewildering to an outsider. You get them to explain to you ('I don't see how those two things join up?', 'You've lost me there' and so on). This kind of probe conveys an important message: that you are listening, that you are trying to make sense; that it is up to *them* to explain things to *you*.

Giving an example

This is a variant of justification. The interviewee will use a term ('confusing', 'irrelevant', 'disruptive') and you say, for example, 'Give me an example' or 'What exactly do you mean when you say that's "irrelevant"?' The trouble is that these shorthand, abstract words mean different things to different people so that interpretation is speculative. A statement like 'He's very aggressive' is open to a wide variety of interpretations; only by asking for an example of the 'aggressiveness' can you determine how it is being used.

Extending the narrative

The mobility of the interview, the number of issues that crop up, the nature of conversation itself, means that sometimes, having embarked on a 'narrative' - an account of something that happened interviewees cut it short as something else occurs to them. Or they feel they have said enough when you can see there is some development there, or some need for further reflection. 'Tell me a bit more about that meeting' or 'What happened after that?' will keep the interviewee going in the direction that he or she had started; you can then decide whether to switch to something else.

Accuracy

For all of us accurate factual recall is a problem: as doctors know, taking a medical history presents special problems because of this. It is not just a matter of dates, or details like that, but also of the *order* of when things happened. One check on this is the *internal consistency* of what people tell you and you can query them on that, e.g. 'I thought that was before you moved to your present post.' Or you can run over the sequence of events, e.g. 'Let me see if I've got things in the right order ...'. It is necessary to remember that the interview can be a source of error: hence the importance of checking your understanding of what has been covered in the closure phase of the interview.

Accuracy of *self-knowledge* is a much more difficult one: people don't always understand their motives and feelings; and their behaviour or history may well contradict what they affirm. This issue is discussed in the Endnote (The Limits of Interview Data).

Reflecting as a special form of probing

Reflecting is the technique of offering back, essentially in the *interviewee's* own words, the essence of what they have just said. This can vary from repeating a 'key' phrase or word to focus the interviewee, to some sort of paraphrasing (perhaps including a reference to the apparent feelings involved), which is more usual.

It is difficult to do well and if it is done in a mechanical way can seem idiotic. As a technique it emerged from 'non-directive' therapeutic approaches, i.e. those based on the assumption that it is clients who have the answers to their problems and the therapist's job is to help them locate and express those personal solutions.

So what it encourages is a form of *self-reflection* that does not depend on a questioning stance on the part of the interviewer or therapist. If it is done effectively it allows interviewees to feel that the formulation that emerges is *theirs* even if they couldn't have got there alone.

The goals of the research interview are not therapeutic, although it is not out of the question that the person being interviewed finds that he or she has learnt something.

Expressing yourself is part of the process of understanding yourself and people can sometimes feel impelled to make disclosures which are startlingly personal. As a researcher, one is not after that sort of material, but it is an index of how people can feel free to talk, even *want* to, at a level which gives you access to material that is normally not expressed at all.

Direct questioning does not easily convey empathy and understanding; and may actually inhibit disclosure. In a sense reflecting does not *add* to what the interviewee has said; but it does two things:

- by summarizing the overt content it focuses the interviewee on the essence of what he or she has just said so as to encourage its further exploration;
- it indicates an awareness of the emotional state behind what has been said.

In other words, it shows that you have been listening carefully, and that you are sensitive to the personal significance of what has been said. How does one achieve this as an interviewer? The answer is *not* to think too much in terms of *technique* (which means focusing on oneself) but to focus hard on the person you are interviewing. If you have a clear grasp of the principle that the *interviewee* owns the content and that your job is to help him or her to express that then the appropriate response will emerge almost naturally.

At this point an example is necessary (see Box 6.1). This example is fictional but it is sufficiently true-to-life to illustrate the different quality of *reflecting* compared with questioning, and how reflecting *builds on* what has been said and keeps things moving in a direction indicated by the interviewee (but still compatible with the overall research aims – in this hypothetical example the difficulties and support experienced by probationary teachers, and the relevance of training).

Reflecting encourages the interviewee to explore further,

Box 6.1

Reflecting at Work

- Well, when I had my first teaching post. . . . Well, no matter how much you prepare you feel 'I've got to get in there and take charge. . . .' One of the classes had the reputation of being, well, not easy . . .
- *You didn't feel you could plan how to control the class.*
- That's right . . . and your training, well, it helped a bit I suppose . . . and the senior staff in the school, well they had a lot to do, always busy. Friendly, you know . . .
- *You didn't think you could get much help from them.*
- I'm not blaming them . . . but, no. But there was another teacher . . . been there years . . . and she said: keep it simple. Do this and do that and that . . . you haven't got time to be subtle . . .
- *Only simple rules could work.*
- Exactly . . . I mean the lecturers at college, would have been shocked! (laughs). But they weren't in there and I was.
- *You're not sure how practically useful your training was.*
- (Pauses) In that respect yes . . .

---

perhaps developing previously uncoordinated elements. This is part of the work of an interview; and is one of the great strengths of the technique.

In questionnaires people are often asked their opinions (with tightly structured ways of responding) but this presumes that people have 'opinions' in a readily accessible and organized form. Quite often this is not the case and it is only in 'discussion' that people can work out and express what they feel or believe. Opinions and feelings are often vague and ill-defined.

This dynamic character of interviewing can be its most fascinating aspect, leading to genuine discovery -- for both parties involved.

7

Piloting and Running the Interview

The pilot interview is an advanced stage of development: close to the real thing. You will have been coming near it as you 'trial' your questions – but that is concerned with getting the *questions* right rather than getting the *interview* right. As we have seen in the preceding chapters, there is a lot more to interviewing than asking questions. And getting these elements essentially how to manage an interview and make it work – under control so that you feel reasonably fluent and confident requires practice.

So we can make a distinction between *practising* interviewing – as a skill and *piloting* the interview so that you can concentrate on the specifics of that and make last minute adjustments and alterations. No matter what work you have put into the different parts of the interview, when it is all put together it is different: adjustments to content are required.

Most of the practising should come before piloting, but they can overlap and combine their functions to some extent. This is also true of *content analysis*: categorizing and sorting what the interviewee has said to you. That is dealt with separately in Chapter 9 because it is a big topic in its own right. But in the chronology of interview development it has to start being practised well in advance of the pilot interview stage.

Content analysis proper comes *after* you have carried out the research interviews (though you transcribe each interview as you go). But if your first experience of the technique is at that stage you are headed for disaster. This is because when you learn what it involves, there is a powerful backwash effect on the construction of the interview, and on the control and management of content.

If you are doing ten interviews and you allow each one to run on for fifteen minutes longer than you intended, then you have added around fifty hours work to your analysis stage.

All these factors have to be carefully weighed when you are putting together your pilot interview.

Your first pilot will have a number of defects that soon become obvious: length is a major problem (as it is with questionnaires). The irresistible temptation is to put in everything you would *like* to ask. At this stage that is no terrible thing: but you have to prune and that means you have to *prioritize* the content.

If you prune for manageability – and length can be a problem for the interviewee as well as for you – then, as you reduce it, you end up with an interview that has more bite and interest. You will find that some overlapping topics can be dispensed with altogether so that the interview is better focused on distinct areas. Questions that are significantly different in character are likely to be more motivating for the interviewee, but also by separating them out in this way your analysis will fall more easily into topic groups, with the main question as a kind of heading.

A well developed interview schedule with a logic to its sequence will usually mean that different interviewees will make similar *kinds* of responses to the questions and this greatly facilitates the process of categorizing. A properly developed and piloted interview helps interviewees to organize themselves, which, in turn, makes things easier for you.

Similarly, if the questions are constructed to deal with relatively distinct *topics*, and if you keep interviewees on course, then categorizing within those topic areas will be correspondingly easier.

The essential point which applies to all empirical research research that is concerned with collecting evidence – is that, in general, you need to have a fairly clear idea of how you are going to analyse the data before you collect them. The procedures you develop for your analysis will affect how you get hold of your data and in what form. As far as possible your data collection should be 'organized' for the later analysis.

Piloting the interview

Piloting proper is a dress rehearsal which includes all the elements of the real thing. But when you have your interview in shape you can do one or two pre-pilots, which are the equivalent of actors reading the parts before a rehearsal proper. You use people who are representative of the group you are researching but not *from* that particular group. And you work through the schedule.

To pursue the acting analogy, this is the point where the need for 'rewriting' becomes apparent. A lot is learnt from this first reality test. *You ask your interviewee for feedback and comments.* But you will learn a lot just from your own experience of it. No matter how experienced you are at research interviewing this first 'reality test' will throw up issues that hadn't occurred to you.

When you are satisfied with the content and structure of the interview *then* you can have your dress rehearsals. It is suggested that you should do at least two of these and that *you should transcribe and content analyse one of them.*

How you do a content analysis is described in the next chapter, but this kind of full content analysis should not be your first experience of the technique. A simple form of practice (using written responses to an open question) is given in that same chapter. Only when you have experienced that should you attempt a fully fledged content analysis.

That will cost you some work; but it will have the effect of saving you a great deal more work.

Analysis and writing up is the most difficult stage of any research. The difficulty is magnified many times if you don't fully appreciate what the analysis involves and requires. It is not just a matter of its being more work than you can manage but, because you haven't developed your material so that it is susceptible to analysis, you end up with the demoralizing experience of having a mass of data that is virtually unanalysable.

It is possible to expend an enormous amount of time transcribing interviews which are of such a sprawling character that content analysis is impossible. In other words, because the researcher did not know where he or she was going with the interviews (requirement one) and did not appreciate what analysis involved (requirement two), the data lacked the kind of focus indispensable for this activity.

Content analysis is a technique which can only be learnt *by doing it*. An 'apprenticeship' role is useful, i.e. working with someone of experience. But it is still essentially a 'self-teaching' experience, and its lessons take a while to be absorbed. That is why you start well in advance of the real thing.

Giving and transcribing the interviews

We have dealt with the organization and management of the interview, so that doesn't need to be repeated here.

The missing element, however, is the *timetabling* of the interviews and transcription. Interviews require a lot of concentration and you will find them a rather wearing business. So space them out. One every two days is about right. This will mean that you can transcribe as you go; and you will find that each interview is relatively fresh in your memory. This makes listening to the tape a lot easier. Easiest of all is if you use headphones and are an expert word-processor; but most of us are not in that league.

You will soon see why a two-day timetable spacing is not too far spread out; it may be that the interval needs to be greater than that.

The point is not just that doing all the transcriptions in one block is a daunting task, but that they will lack the freshness in your mind that makes 'hearing' easier. If you have to listen too hard (and we are not now talking particularly about the recording *quality*) then the task can become very wearing. The converse applies: if the recording quality is not brilliant, 'recency' will make hearing easier.

Simple efficiency is also an essential: dating and identifying your tapes; storing them properly; perhaps making back-up copies. Lost or mislaid tapes, like lost or mislaid computer disks, are an all too common occurrence. Your research data are central.

8

Carrying out a Content Analysis

Content analysis is about organizing the *substantive* content of
the interview: the content that is of substance. So there are
two essential strands to the analysis:

- identifying those key, substantive points;
- putting them into categories.

'Categories' are simply headings – a first stage in tidily
presenting the range of data the interviews have thrown up.
In themselves those headings don't amount to much: the
substance and meaning come with the use of direct quotations categorized in this way but displaying the range and
character of the responses. Choosing and identifying categories is a subjective business but not an idiosyncratic one:
a 'sensible' way of ordering the data. Arriving at categories
is troublesome and time-consuming but not otherwise
difficult.

Identifying substantive statements

Identifying substantive statements is easier than one
might expect (although you need to check that your subjective impressions or judgements agree with another
person's independent judgements – see later). The most
striking thing about transcribed speech (and which makes

transcription an onerous business) is that most of what people say is redundant: a river of words in which the real substance floats along more or less conspicuously. If this reads like a harsh judgement then the experience of transcription and analysis will show it to be largely true. The simple truth is that none of us speak like a tightly edited written text: the effect would be inhuman if we did. Repetition, for example, is tiresome in written text but necessary for emphasis and elaboration when we are speaking. This is particularly true when people are 'thinking on their feet' — working mentally on the topic that has been presented to them to deal with.

Written text has been cleaned up and condensed: not a problem when readers can stop to think about what they have just read. Print doesn't move along like speech: you can go back and re-read if necessary. And so on.

So uncharitable thoughts about a prolix interviewee need to be tempered with this kind of awareness. You are reducing discourse of an exploratory nature to written text.

Constructing categories

The overall purpose of constructing categories is to be able to assign all the 'substantive' statements to them: you don't want to throw any of these away — they are going to be the meat of your write-up. If you find that you have 'left-over' or unique statements you can still present them, commenting on their possible value or significance, perhaps in an 'unclassifiable' category.

So a requirement for the derivation of categories is that they should be *exhaustive*. But another requirement is that they should be *exclusive*, i.e. that the kind of statements that go into one category clearly belong there and couldn't really go anywhere else.

This relates back to the point made in Chapter 3 (focusing

on the interview questions) that different questions should cover different topics. This aids later analysis because it requires the interviewee to 'move on' to talk about something else.

The process of developing and combining (or breaking up) categories is essentially about observing the principles of exhaustiveness and exclusiveness. And both requirements become impossible unless you have developed and focused the interview properly.

Is transcription really necessary?

There are short cuts. One is to listen to the tape and note down the substantive statements as they float along the stream of consciousness. There is a good deal of to-ing and fro-ing with the tape and, when you have abstracted the statements, you need to run through the tape again, listening for anything you might have missed. You also need to double-check by asking someone else to do the same exercise (without sight of your list) to see if he or she identifies the same statements. This needs to be reported in your write-up, and you have to judge what to do about 'disagreements'.

The main weakness of this technique is that you end up with a lot of rather disconnected statements because you have lost their context. This causes you to reconsider the value of the 'redundant' material: without it the key statements lose some of their meaning and significance.

Actually this technique works best when you are using it as a preliminary for developing the set of questions for a questionnaire (see pp. 20–1 in *Developing a Questionnaire*). But if it is a physical impossibility to do a proper transcription analysis, then it is a great deal better than doing without this kind of data altogether.

The content analysis of transcribed interviews

You can't really study an interview's content except in complete written form; and that involves writing down everything, including the main questions you ask, and the prompts and probes you use – supplementary questions in effect. Without these you won't make complete sense of what the interviewee has said (it is like listening in to one end of a telephone conversation). Moreover, your main questions are like sub-headings which sectionalize the interview for purposes of content analysis – although it is not quite as tidy as that.

The style of word-processing a transcription is important. Content analysis is a task requiring a great deal of concentration and you need to make it easy for yourself. These are the key points:

1. Don't put too many words on a page – around 350 is about right. This means double-spacing with generous margins (which you will need for notes or coding references).
2. Use a different typeface for your questions/interjections, so that what the *interviewee* says is clearly demarcated. If you use bold for your own *main* questions that also marks the 'headings'. You can italicize your other probes and prompts.
3. Clearly identify each transcript, whether by name, other details or code.

A one-hour interview is going to yield about 5,000–6,000 words of *interview* material; at around 350 words to a page that's about 18 pages per transcript. This is your raw material. To get it into shape you have to be highly systematic: an interesting but tiring business. In summary this is how you go about it:

1. Take each transcript in turn.
2. Go through each one highlighting substantive statements (those that really make a point). Ignore repetitions, digressions and other clearly irrelevant material.
3. Some statements will be similar but if you feel they 'add something' mark them up.
4. Take a break. If you try to do transcripts one after another your concentration will become dulled. Two a day, well spaced, is a maximum. But don't space them *too* much or you will lose the categories that will be forming in your mind.
5. When you have been through all the transcripts go back to the first one and read them through again. Are there any statements you have failed to highlight? Have you highlighted some that aren't really 'substantive'? It may be useful to ask someone else to go through a set of unmarked transcripts, highlighting what he or she sees as 'substantive' statements as a check on your judgement. Make any changes necessary.
6. Now comes the difficult, intellectually creative stage. You go back to the beginning again (after an interval!) and, going through the highlighted statements, try to derive a set of categories for the responses to each question. Give these a simple heading ('Safety training procedures', 'Experiences of playground bullying', 'Getting advice on benefit claims' and so on). At this point all you are trying to do is construct a list of category headings. You will get a lot from the first transcript, more from the next but progressively fewer as you work through them all, because individuals will be making essentially similar points. Depending on the number of categories you are deriving, you may find it easier to go from one transcript to another dealing with one main question at a time. If you have more than half a dozen interviews you almost certainly need to do it this way.

7. You then look at your list of categories and ask yourself whether some of them could be combined or, alternatively, split up. As you are compiling the list you will sense that some of the headings you have noted down are not adequate or necessary. There is more work to be done here.

8. Go through the transcripts, with your list of categories beside you. Check each *substantive* (highlighted) statement against the category list to see if it has somewhere to go. Mark '?' by those statements you cannot readily assign to any category. Modify the wording of the category headings (or revise them entirely) so that they fit the statements better or can include 'query' statements. It may be that you will need to add new categories. If there are a lot of 'query' statements then you should deal with them at a separate stage: too many of these may indicate that your list of category headings is inadequate *or* that you have a lot of 'unique' statements that necessarily resist classification: see below.

9. Enter your categories on an analysis grid like the one in Figure 8.1. If you have a large number of categories for each question, make up a grid or spreadsheet for each of them rather than for the transcripts as a whole. The category headings go along the top, the names or codes of the respondents down the side. If you make the analysis sheets A3 size (or even larger) you will be able to enter in the cells what the respondents actually said, or part of it. This is very useful when you come to write up. Category headings, remember, are simply a way of classifying the kinds of statements people have made: they don't tell you much on their own.

10. Go through the transcripts, assigning each substantive statement (where possible) to a category. Statements you can't assign have to be dealt with separately: 'unclassifiable' but *not* unimportant. Sometimes just one

Categories

Respondents	1	2	3	4	5	6	etc.
1							
2							
3							
4							
5							
6							
7							
8							
9							
10							
11							
12							
etc							

Figure 8.1. An analysis grid.

individual makes a key point. Put the *number* of the category against the statement on the transcript: this tells you that you have entered it and where it has gone; if you can't classify a statement mark it u.c. (unclassifiable). On the analysis grid you can either *tick* the relevant box (this person made a statement which fits this category) or *write in the actual statement*, or you can *do both* on separate sheets: one for a *count* analysis (how many people said this kind of thing) and one for a *meaning* analysis. Sometimes a count analysis is all that is required, but tabulating the actual statements has a lot to recommend it: it brings the summary category to life, conveys the *range* of responses that come under it and provides material for the qualitative analysis write-up that comes later. And even if you do just 'tick the box' you need to make a note of 'exemplar' quotes for each category. These categories can have a bland, uniform quality and, in a sense 'lose' a lot of information; you need to be able to bring them to life.

11. With your interviews analysed in this fashion you have the material for the final analysis and write-up. That final stage is dealt with in the next chapter.

A first practical exercise

Reading through the procedure outlined above may make content analysis seem a daunting task. It does involve a lot of work, but it is not intrinsically difficult; and if you start at a much simpler level it becomes a feasible proposition.

In a parallel volume in this series, entitled *Developing a Questionnaire*, a practical exercise is described for content analysing the *written* responses to open questions (pp. 66-9). Questionnaires are composed almost entirely of *closed* questions where the choice of answers is prescribed, so that 'analysis' is built in. However, a *very small* number of open questions is often useful in questionnaires (e.g. 'Do you have any comments to make about our service that haven't been covered by the preceding questions?').

The process of analysing these sorts of answers is essentially the same as that for an interview, except that:

- you don't have to transcribe (it is written for you);
- there is much less material because people are less prolix when they write than when they talk.

So it is a simpler task. And because it is simpler it enables you to practise the most difficult part of content analysis: deriving categories that fit the range of different responses from a number of different individuals.

The exercise the author uses with his students (about 10–12 in number in any one course) is to ask them to write down what they see as the positive and negative features of the course. When they have done this each individual's written response is photocopied so that each student has a complete set of *all* the responses: which they then have to analyse, following more or less the procedures outlined earlier.

Because what is required is well defined, this analysis is not a difficult exercise, but it is difficult enough and it inducts novices into the central task of content analysis. It also exemplifies the point made that *you learn content analysis by doing it.*

If you are on a course you can do the same kind of thing. If you are not you could do something very similar with your co-professionals (for example, 'What are the positive and negative aspects of working in this hospital, school, police force . . .?').

It can be repeated here (and cannot be repeated too often) that poorly developed research instruments (observation schedules, questionnaires, interviews) only reveal their full inadequacies when you come to the stage of analysis.

But this kind of warning only has impact when you engage in preparatory practice of the kind just described. When you see what is involved in content analysing ten people's written response (perhaps on one side of A4 – and you can set this as a requirement) to a straightforward and well focused question, then you can see quite clearly what would be involved in the analysis of ten interview transcriptions of answers to six main questions and covering fifteen pages or more each. And that would be a fairly tidy outcome. A sprawling uncontrolled set of interviews would involve much more.

But we need to step back from practicalities altogether for a while and consider the conceptual issues involved in analysis.

The origins of content analysis

Content analysis originated in the USA at the beginning of the twentieth century, as an essentially *quantitative* technique for analysing the balance of content of newspapers, i.e. the proportion of 'serious' news coverage, etc. This is easily measured, even in the literal sense of column inches and of course as a proportion of total coverage. Although there is some subjectivity in deciding what is 'serious', the *kind* of content (so much on sport, so much on home news, etc.) is relatively objective.

This 'count' style of content analysis is widely used across all media (violence or explicit sex scenes on television; the depiction of minority or disadvantaged groups; gender imbalance and representation; and so on). One could, for example, do an analysis of textbooks to see how they used gender pronouns. (Is 'he' used more often than 'she'? Are gender-specific pronouns avoided?) For these kinds of analyses computers, and specialist software, are highly appropriate.

Low inference and high inference content analysis

What has been described above is the content analysis of what is more or less on the *surface*, where descriptive categories can be formed with very little inference being involved.

The trouble is that if you want to construct a *meaningful* analysis of what people have said, to construct categories which bring together what they have expressed in different ways, you have to make judgements about *latent* meaning, i.e. what they 'meant' by what they said. This is nothing more than the easily understood notion that people can 'mean' the same thing, or say things of the same kind, but using very different words and forms of expression. In other words, a 'surface' analysis wouldn't form the kind of meaningful category that might be appropriate.

At this point the issues are becoming rather abstract so we need to give some concrete examples. Let us suppose that in the analysis of interviews with young unemployed people you derive the category *Perceived attitudes of potential employers*. Statements you might include here could be:

- 'You could tell he wasn't really interested. He'd said it all before a hundred times. Very polite ... but it didn't mean anything.'
- 'Well, I got there on time ... and I waited ... and then this woman came out ... she said Mrs Evans is in a meeting. Could you come back?'
- 'They answered my letter right away ... a proper letter ... an interview and they said to ring in for an appointment to suit me.'

These are fictional examples, of course, but they make the point that the *manifest* content is quite different in each case but the *latent* content can meaningfully be identified as bearing on the same theme.

Categories at this level reflect properties of the human

mind. They are not 'objective' any more than human values are 'objective', and different people may arrive at different categories. But the essential argument is whether the categories make sense to the reader as a way of organizing and presenting the content of the interviews. Such categories are always, to some extent, a matter of personal judgement, which is why, when you are presenting your analysis, the *actual category content statements* should be comprehensively presented. The reader can then see what was meant by the category heading and decide whether or not he or she disagrees. *Category labels or headings on their own don't mean very much.* Indeed, presented as such they may be positively misleading because the reader will *attribute* his or her own interpretation.

The basic tenet underlying what has been written here is that if you don't make inferences you can make no progress in understanding, *but the essential basis for your inferences must be made explicit.*

Categories and subjectivity

Although this issue is a fundamental one, it has been left to last in this chapter because without a run-through of the practicalities it would appear excessively abstract. It is in fact a philosophical issue fundamental to knowledge. And it is this.

Categories are formed in the human brain: they are a product of, and a characteristic of, human intelligence. They are not an objective property of objects: classification of birds, animals, insects, flowers, trees and shrubs is a major preoccupation of the relevant sciences. They are conventions, no matter how 'rationally' based. Even at a more superficial level there is uncertainty (when does a shrub become a tree, for example?).

Now physical objects are relatively 'low inference' compared with human behaviour, feelings, motives and the like. Yet these elements may be fundamental to classifying what people say in an interview.

Take the statements quoted on p. 69 as evidence of 'perceived attitudes of potential employers'. The category makes sense but it could be described as 'positive and negative experiences in seeking employment' or, arguably, 'poor self-esteem of young people seeking employment'. All make some kind of sense.

What this means is that:

- we cannot achieve 'definitive' categories;
- category headings, *by themselves*, cannot convey the essential character of the statements so classified.

It follows from this that we must have this in the forefront of our mind when we are writing up our interview findings.

One can exaggerate this point. Because we share a common intellectual culture we will *tend* to form similar kinds of categories to other people, but we need to ask for peer review of our analysis so that we can be challenged on points where our 'category construction' is perhaps not doing justice to the content.

'Peer review' — getting someone equally competent to yourself (perhaps more competent?) — is also relevant at a more basic level: the initial identification of substantive statements. You will have been through your transcripts highlighting these 'significant' statements. But the judgement is again a subjective one and because it is basic to the whole exercise it is a critical one.

What you do is to give an unmarked transcript to your 'peer', explain the nature of your research and ask him or her to highlight what *he or she* sees as the substantive statements. What you typically find is that there are large agreements. What is of value is where your peer has *not* highlighted statements that *you* identified and, perhaps more important, has highlighted statements that you didn't.

This double-checking is an essential part of the rigour of your analysis, and needs to be reported as part of your procedure. You don't have to accept your peer's judgement as the correct one. Instead, you use it as a basis for *reviewing your own judgements*. Typically, you find you accept some of the 'disagreements' but not others. That is perfectly acceptable, the essential point being that you have *sought* that kind of validation of your judgements.

Asking someone to parallel your categorical analysis is rarely feasible or reasonable; if you *evidence* your categories and acknowledge their fundamental subjectivity that is usually enough.

9

Writing up Interview Data

The great virtue of a rigorous content analysis is that it immerses you in the *detail* of your substantive findings. The process of classifying and categorizing, difficult though it is, has a disciplining effect not just on your spreadsheets but on your own intellectual grasp of your material.

This organization has the effect of enabling you to *see* more clearly the significance, particularly the general significance, of what people have said to you. Your mind will, therefore, have been working on two levels: the task of *categorization* and the task of *interpretation*. The interesting thing about the latter is that it is a process that goes on without any prompting from you. At the end of Chapter 8 we said that categorization is characteristic of human intelligence, but so also is *interpretation*: it is part of the everyday process of living. And by the same token it is not entirely a self-conscious or even a conscious activity. When you are dealing with a wide range of rather complicated information there is a good deal of unconscious work of this kind. *And you have to allow time for this unconscious process to operate.*

This is just as well. Having carried out a comprehensive content analysis you will feel the need for a break. A two-week interval will not be wasted, because at the end of that time you will come back to your material with a fresh eye and a *better organized mind* for the writing-up process.

Getting down to the business of writing

An organized mind still needs organized material - and, of course, to a large extent the former emerges from the activity of constructing the latter.

Let us review the process of organizing your data. It started at the level of question development – identifying questions of real importance that are likely to call forth an interested response on the part of the interviewee. If there is substance in the question there will be substance in the answers to it. And if each question deals with a different topic there will be a discernible difference in substance between them.

So when you come to write up your material (the quotations you are going to use) your organization is there in a readily accessible format, at two levels: the main question you posed, which you can treat as a *main heading* – perhaps a section or even a chapter; and your categories, which you can treat as sub-headings.

Since you have coded your quotations on the spreadsheets to the specific transcripts they come from, you can refer back to them if you need more 'context' at the point of writing up.

Writing up

The essential character of writing up interview data is to weave a narrative which is interpolated with illustrative quotes. Your task is essentially to allow the interviewees to speak for themselves, with linking material which does little more than ensure continuity and point up the import of what the interviewees are saying. A good example of this is the study of single lone mothers by Burghes and Brown, previously cited. A more extended quotation is given in Box 9.1, exemplifying exactly the points that have just been made.

74

Box 9.1

Other help

Other sources of help mentioned by the single lone mothers included a local family centre, a foster mother and other mothers living in the same hostel.

'I was quite lucky ... even though I didn't have support from my family ... I were in a hostel for young mothers when I first had J ... we all rallied round together ... they helped me a lot ... told me about their experiences about bringing up a baby.'

Four mothers also referred specifically to help from their boyfriends' mothers, while two cited support received from the boyfriends themselves. Grandparents and friends were also mentioned, sometimes as part of the assistance received from an extended family consortium:

'... his sister ... used to come over and talk to me. She used to stay in the house with me till him or his mum came back from work so it weren't so bad ... she either watches him or me mum watches him or S watches him when I go out.'

'... I had all my friends and they helped me.... My mum, my auntie and then my cousins would come and take him out and things like that.'

'I was living with a full family so there was a lot of help there. So it'd probably be a totally different story if I was on my own.'

Sometimes, however, support from extended family and friends had not lasted beyond an initial burst of enthusiasm following the birth:

'... for the first six months of having her it was fine ... people were very willing to babysit for a new baby; but then when it got to the teething stage, the friends disappeared.'

'... When I had her I had a lot of help but now she's one ... they don't want to know. And it seems harder for me all the time.'

You don't include *all* the relevant quotes - just enough to give the range and variety of the answers. And if there are 'discrepant' quotes you add them as a qualifying insight. You can see how Burghes and Brown have done this.

Quantitative analyses

One way in which you can reflect the *generality* of the kinds of statements quoted is to cite how many of the interviewees made that point (or one like it) or how many made different or contradictory points. Burghes and Brown make an observation of this kind in their connecting narrative in Box 9.1. That is usually sufficient but there are occasions, i.e. when the picture is a little more complicated, to set out the different pattern of statements in a tabular form. If it is easier to 'see' the point like that then it is justified. Numerical relationships are sometimes clumsily expressed in verbal form.

The balance of quotation and linking narrative

It goes without saying that the quotations you select should be *representative* of the total range. Some people will have made the same point in a more vivid or compelling way than others; and, of course, you should select those. What you have to guard against is selecting quotations that suit your particular preferences or present a neater picture. The best lies are half-truths and carefully selected quotations can totally distort the picture. An honest balance has to be struck there.

An equally important balance is that between quotations and the *amount* of linking narrative. An approximate practical guide is that quotations should make up not less than a third of the text, but not more than half.

Under the category sub-headings you will need an introductory paragraph or two, but then you should let the interviewees take over, with no more than a meaningful linking between the quotations – and sometimes you should simply cite several in succession.

This linking should be like a *framework* that holds the quotations together – but it is these (what your interviewees have *said*) which should make the point. In terms of *emphasis*, the material should be 90 per cent from the interviewees.

Reviewing your selection of quotations

We have already cautioned against the risks of 'selective bias' - selecting to favour a particular emphasis. That is not necessarily a consciously corrupt process, but you have to guard against it all the same.

Your selection may be unbalanced for no malign reasons whatsoever. There can be a 'drift' in the quotations that catch your attention when you are writing up, which results in a completely unintended bias. How does one guard against that?

The basic procedure is a simple one. You have your spreadsheets with the category headings and the columns of statements from individual interviews. As you *use* a quotation in your write-up you should highlight it. That tells you which ones you have used and which ones you have chosen not to. At various points you should scan the selected and non-selected quotations to check your justification for your choice. What you are after is a *balanced* representation. Some of them will make the 'representative' points better than others. However, there may be shades or nuances that are not caught by just one or two quotations.

How many quotations?

There are two main determinants here. If all or most of your interviewees have made the same kind of point then the *commonality* of this needs to be demonstrated by a range of quotations: one in isolation might convey the incorrect message that it was a 'one off', although you should or could indicate that *x* number of people said essentially the same thing. But the number of quotations is still part of the impact of *quality*.

The second point is that although people may be saying *approximately* the same kind of thing there will be shades of opinions, important variations of detail which can only be conveyed by a range of quotations. In a sense these statements are 'unpacking' what the category heading signifies. When you scan the highlighted items on your spreadsheet you may find that you have been too selective. It has to be borne in mind that you identified these initially as having 'something to say'. If they don't add anything to other quotations then it is perfectly fair to omit them. But you have to justify that choice to yourself and to others.

Basic to the kind of research that semi-structured interviews are a part of is the *trustworthiness* of procedures. This means more than being honest and checking that your data are sound, and acknowledging their limits. It also means that the processes, like data analysis, are open for inspection. This kind of open accounting is part of what E.G. Guba and Y.S. Lincoln (1981) in *Effective Evaluation*, San Francisco: Jossey-Bass, call the 'audit trail' – a trail that someone else, the 'auditor', can follow to see how you reached your conclusions.

Quite apart from the integrity issue, by documenting or preserving the records of your process of analysis you can, if necessary, *backtrack* to check on your chain of evidence and the reasoning derived from that.

In the same way that traditionally 'scientific' quantitative researchers might check back on their calculations (because the results are of a level that raise questions), so naturalistic researchers may need to review the 'calculations' that led them to draw the conclusions they have.

All researchers must expect to be challenged on their findings: your justification is only as good as the means by which you achieved them.

As we have said before, data do not just speak for themselves: selection and interpretation *are* required but these should be kept to the minimum necessary for the implications of the evidence to be apparent.

10

Special Interviewing Techniques

There are different kinds of research interviews, and if we have focused on the one which is of most general application, that does not mean that other techniques are not valuable in particular instances.

The 'elite' interview

You may not like the word 'elite' but the term is common currency to researchers using interview techniques: it has a special meaning.

Often in an institution or profession there is someone (or a small number of people) who is in a privileged position as far as *knowledge* is concerned; no doubt in other ways too. These are often people in positions of authority, with considerable personal power. But it may be that they are just particularly expert or authoritative and so are members of an 'elite' in that sense.

Although they may be remote from some aspects of what you are researching, they are likely to have a particularly comprehensive grasp of the wider context, and to be privy to information that is withheld from others. Quite simply, their perspective is different.

So you could be dealing with a company director, a senior hospital administrator, the director of an art school, a head-teacher; or a specialist academic, a veteran designer or someone retired from professional practice but with a view that has both length and breadth.

This is a very varied group but all the examples are characterized by the possession of a great deal more knowledge than you about their area, the topic and its setting. They will also have the characteristics that long authority gives people – in particular, that they will not submit to being tamely 'interviewed', where you direct a series of questions at them.

It is not just that they have acquired the habit of being 'in control', though that is part of it; it is more that in some respects they know better which questions you should be asking and, at a more profound level, how knowledge of the subject is best organized. So, for all these reasons, you have to expect them to take charge to some extent.

They will also expect to have some control over what you are doing, and to require a degree of accountability – reporting back, consulting with them on delicate issues (which they will usually indicate).

If you can accept this level of control (and you probably have little choice) they can be uniquely informative, as well as facilitating your research activities.

All this means is that, from your point of view, the interview will be relatively unstructured; but in fact the structure will be determined much more by the 'interviewee' (the inverted commas are entirely appropriate here). If you can go along with this (without losing sight of your research aims) you can derive unique benefits.

What exactly can you get out of this kind of interview?

1. The distinctive views and perspective of that individual – to which you can then relate other kinds of evidence that you acquire.
2. Breadth and depth of information: others in the 'system'

may not know fully the background context of what they experience.

3. Guidance on things to look out for, questions you *should* be asking.
4. Hidden snags and sensibilities in the system that you will be largely unaware of, but which are meat and drink to a 'manager'.
5. Where, and what kind of, documents and records can be found; and the permission to gain access to these.
6. The identity of key people you should consult, inside or outside the setting in which you are operating.
7. The relationship between the 'formal' and the 'informal' aspects of the system: managers know the value of, and the complex relationships between, these components — and they have to take account of both. So do you.

An elite interview is something you should report very fully. By its very character it is not susceptible to a 'common themes' content analysis. It is, in any case, more central both in terms of the authority of the evidence and in the role it plays in *directing* your research.

Of course, you edit and summarize, but there should be extensive direct quotation, especially of those statements you want to cross-refer to other kinds of evidence, or which are key indicators for your research direction.

There is a power balance to be struck. If your 'elite interviewee' supports you then that will make life easier for you. However, if you are seen as his or her particular *ally*, that could put a distance between you and others. There are no precise rules for dealing with that; but you need to communicate that you are even-handed in your dealings and are not a retailer of confidences.

What you can sometimes usefully do is to develop a kind of 'consultative' relationship with the individual concerned (a form of control, it has to be acknowledged). In any case, a follow-up interview later in your investigation, where you can present your findings and raise further queries, will almost certainly be productive.

Video interviewing

We have discussed the use of video as part of your personal training programme. However, your actual research interviews will usually be tape-recorded and analysed as transcribed text. But it is equally possible to *video* your research interviews, though there is usually more reluctance on the part of the people you want to interview. Setting up a video session is easy with modern equipment, and especially if you have a specially designed 'studio' – common in some settings.

But why would you do it? It mainly depends on what you want to use the video-taped 'material' for. Video gives you greater impact by including the element of *non-verbal* communication as well as the physical context of the interview.

We have mentioned above how vivid verbatim quotation can be. But it can be even more vivid if you can see *and* hear the person saying it.

It largely depends on how you are going to present your findings. If, for example, you are going to make use of lecture or seminar formats then *some* video excerpts may add greatly to the impact of the points you are making. However, these need to be very carefully chosen for their relevance because research interviews are rarely compellingly watchable for more than a very few minutes, i.e. you can *lose* impact rather than gain it.

What you have to balance is the trouble of videoing the interview(s) and the use you will make of them. There are two uses that *do* justify the effort:

• Using the video for training in research interviewing; but this presupposes that your interview is some kind of useful model. Interviewing is by and large a private activity.

You don't often get the chance to see anybody doing it – hence the value of studying a practised interviewer at work.

- When your research interest is *particularly* concerned with the *non-verbal* aspects of communication.

A final point is that video interviews are often easier to *transcribe* – because you get supportive meaning from the visual dimension and, if you wish, you can enter in the transcription some of the visual 'communication', e.g. the interviewee's manner as he or she was speaking. This may add to the value and significance of your material.

Telephone interviewing

Telephone interviewing is an attempt to gain some of the qualities of face-to-face interviewing – in particular its flexibility and responsiveness – without the time and money costs of arranging physical meetings. US researchers have been the leaders in this technique, which is largely a phenomenon of the past decade or so.

It is widely used in market research, where cost is an overriding consideration (clients want the most for the least), and is usually both more structured and shorter than the face-to-face semi-structured interview. However, it has also had extensive use, again particularly in the USA, in 'academic' research, and this has included such sensitive topics as early experiences of sexual abuse. Not surprisingly, there is a high refusal rate to such approaches (or a high agreement rate, depending on one's perspective in such matters).

With widely dispersed subjects, e.g. nationally from a 'probability' sample, its advantages are obvious. In a day one could interview half-a-dozen people that it would take several days to visit in person.

Telephone interviewing is often used 'cold', i.e. without

prior agreement or preparation; and the 'probability' or random sample may be reached by 'random digit dialling'. In a society where unsolicited telephone sales approaches are a contemporary nuisance, you have to be particularly skilled, or particularly thick-skinned, to overcome the initial confusion or resistance of the person you are calling.

The better approach, and arguably the ethically more acceptable, is to use telephone interviewing only with people who have given prior agreement and who are clear as to the *purposes* of the interview. It may well be that people are too busy to make an appointment during office hours and don't want to be visited at home, but are perfectly willing to talk on the telephone in the evening or at the weekend.

Telephone interviewing is harder to keep going than the face-to-face variety, and for a corresponding reason people find it harder work. Twenty to thirty minutes is probably a maximum duration unless you have a particularly charismatic telephone manner, and this means you have to be very clear and focused on what you want to ask. The absence of the non-verbal dimension is soon apparent.

Doing a telephone interview makes one aware of how important non-verbal communication is. The difficulty of keeping it going is a reflection of this: you have to rely heavily on your voice – and this is a tiring business because a telephone interview is not like the loose to-and-fro of an ordinary telephone conversation with someone you know well.

One practical support is to *send* interviewees a list of the main questions you want to ask. If you don't want them to 'prepare' too much you can (perhaps) fax this through just before the start of the interview. Those being interviewed usually find it helpful (because structuring) to have something on paper in front of them so that they are not just relying on what is coming down the telephone. And because *they* find it helpful, indirectly that takes some of the burden off you.

Great concentration is required, so you need to be well prepared, but the essential structure is as described in Chapter 5.

The pace of a telephone interview and the difficulty of keeping it going usually mean that it is essential to *record* the telephone conversation – something which your interviewee needs to be aware of. With modern technology this is easier than tape-recording a normal face-to-face interview but usually requires specialist equipment. However, some top-of-the-range answering machines have a two-way recording facility. Models and technology are changing all the time but your telephone company or a specialist telephone retailer will be able to advise you on what is currently available.

Group interviewing

This is a technique which can be very useful early on in your research when you are still finding your way. It is also a means of *communicating* the purposes of your research and raising group awareness of it.

Initially you may be uncertain of your research orientation and you can express this uncertainty by indicating your broad aims and raising issues – in the form of open questions – and seeing what turns up. The group will often do much of the work for you, although some 'chairing' on your part will be necessary, particularly if the discussion gets side-tracked by personal disputes. But conflicts and tensions can themselves be informative, at least at the level of your awareness that there is wider disagreement, or greater sensitivity, than you had anticipated. This is something that may surface more readily in a group than in the calmer atmosphere of an individual interview. Conflict, like crisis, can be very revealing.

Attention to *group composition* is important. One of the interesting things about observing groups at work in this fashion is the way in which differences in *status* are manifested. 'High status' individuals may or may not have the most to say, but they can still dominate the proceedings by inhibiting others. Indeed, their very silence may be more powerful than speech because of the others' uncertainty as to what they are thinking. Even if you don't know abut the differences in formal status you can usually identify those individuals who are perceived as 'high status' in the group by their more relaxed manner – lounging in their chair, for example. It is permitted of them.

There are other factors than status, including gender and age group. Women or men may be inhibited if they are in a marked minority or, in certain respects, if they are in a *majority*. Younger members of staff may be constrained by the presence of some of their elders, with their known sensibilities and so on.

What happens in a group 'interview' is difficult to record, and what emerges may be fragmentary in character; but these elements may become apparent in no other way. Just as in 'family therapy', it may bring out tensions and reveal groupings that would not be manifested in an individual interview.

Recording schedules

These are highly structured and, as we have said above, essentially verbally administered questionnaires.

So why go to the trouble of administering verbally? The answer is that it overcomes two serious weaknesses of questionnaires:

- a low response rate;
- incomplete or 'misunderstood' responses.

If the needs of your research are such that these defects would seriously undermine its validity then you should use recording schedules, rather than questionnaires. 'Live' administration also ensures that what you get is standardized, i.e. all given in the same way.

If you keep them very short, i.e. no more than about ten minutes of 'recording time' and highly structured, then you can accumulate a lot of data in a few days of effort.

The value of this kind of approach is evident in the swarms of market researchers who are to be found in our main shopping streets. Indeed, you can get some idea of what is involved by your experience of these encounters. Factual data plus straightforward 'closed question' opinions are what are best gathered in this fashion.

Depending on what you are researching you can ape these kinds of researchers very exactly. One of the author's undergraduate students stood outside Marks & Spencer taking shoppers through a schedule dealing with their opinions on the disciplining of children.

However, it is not something where you can use the kind of open questions that require an expanded response. Unfortunately, it is not a practicable alternative to the semi-structured interview. It is different in kind; but, in certain circumstances, it is better than nothing.

Endnote: The Limits of
Interview Data

In a book which has expatiated on the richness of interview material and the insight that it can provide into human lives, it is important to end with a cautionary note.

We can all accept that people may be inaccurate in what they tell you about factual events concerning themselves; we can all recognize our own fallibility in that direction. How long have you lived where you do? How many job changes have you had? How much do you spend annually on clothes? And so on.

But there is a general assumption that we 'know ourselves': that we can give a uniquely valid account of how we feel, of how we typically behave or what we intend to do. Who knows better than ourselves, for example, whether – and to what extent – we are satisfied with our lives?

A lot of interview or questionnaire topics, especially in market research – but also in government research of one kind or another – are focused on whether people are satisfied with their life situation or the services they receive.

But if people *say* they are satisfied with their lot, and even if they *believe* what they say, we should still ask: are they *really* satisfied? Which is to say: does other evidence bear this out? This fundamental query bears on the issue of how well people, speaking sincerely in an interview, really know themselves.

The notion of 'satisfaction' is addressed in a paper by the

American sociologist Barbara Gutek ('Strategies for Studying Client Satisfaction', *Journal of Social Issues*, vol. 34, no. 4 (1978), pp. 44–56). Reviewing the literature, she points to studies of 'job satisfaction' where that expression is not strongly related to more *behavioural* measures of dissatisfaction, e.g. absenteeism and job turnover. She goes on to say:

The job satisfaction literature is not unique in finding that people report high levels of satisfaction. Although the 'quality of life' literature is newer, the results being disseminated show the same high levels of satisfaction with life in general and with specific domains of life. For example, Campbell et al. (1976) found that among their nation-wide sample of adults, 22% reported complete satisfaction with their lives, while 39% of respondents were in the next category. On a seven-point scale, only 7% of respondents were below the midpoint. On a question about satisfaction with life, Andrews and Withey (1976) obtained similar results. On a seven-point satisfaction scale, only 6% of people placed themselves below the midpoint. Similar results are obtained when respondents are asked not about life as a whole but about specific domains of their life. For example, 92% of respondents are satisfied with their marriages, including 66% who say they are completely satisfied. Seventy percent are satisfied with their health, 75% are satisfied with their living standard, and 73% are satisfied with their house or apartment. The Gallup organization, attempting to assess satisfaction globally, also reports very high levels of satisfaction in the United States, but lower rates in other areas of the world, especially in third world countries (Gallup, 1976 1977).

Gutek concludes: 'One reason for distrusting measures of satisfaction is simply that people seem to be satisfied with everything that social scientists ask them about.'

Now one has to be cautious about drawing too extensive an inference here. The studies Gutek refers to used *questionnaires* and *rating scales* of the 'very satisfied' to 'very dissatisfied' variety. One of the limitations of these scales is that people tend not to use the negative end of the scale, or only to a limited extent; especially when they apply to trivial matters of judgement (e.g. seating comfort on an aeroplane). To some extent, therefore, these findings may be an artefact of method.

But the general point that Gutek makes is of importance and the implication for assessing the validity of interview data is that interviews need to be part of a *multi-method* approach, like case studies (see pp. 21–3 of the parallel volume in this series, *Case Study Research Methods*).

Of course, one can take the stance that interviewing gives you access to a person's *subjective* world and that 'objective' phenomena are about something else. It is evident that they must be, but it reflects on the meaning of subjective expression that objective expression is at variance. Clearly the relationship is not straightforward.

What people give as their opinion is one thing; statements about behaviour are quite another. If what people say in an interview is presumed (by the researcher or the interviewer) to bear some sort of direct relation to what the interviewee actually *does* or *would do*, then we need to treat that assumption as equally questionable.

We commonly have quite explicit *intentions* of what we are going to do in a given situation, but actually behave in a quite different way. Quite simply, we may not know ourselves as well as we think, or behave as we would like to think we behave. Words and deeds are not the same; nor, it should be added, are beliefs and deeds.

The misunderstanding of the relationship between what we say, believe or know and what we *do* is pervasive – so pervasive, indeed, that it often goes unquestioned.

The emphasis in our time on health and social education is a case in point. Social problems such as teenage pregnancy, drug abuse, smoking and unhealthy diet are commonly 'tackled' in this way, often at great public expense. But such approaches are predicated on the assumption that if people *know* the risks involved, or what they *should* do, they will change their behaviour. Would that it were so simple; because when these approaches are evaluated they are typically shown to have no, or a very limited, effect. For example, a colleague in the Department of Psychology at Strathclyde University was involved in the development and evaluation of a secondary school drug education programme. It was a considerable success: teachers were enthusiastic about it, the young people learnt a great deal about the risks and nature of drug abuse. However, on follow-up it was shown to have had absolutely no effect on drug-taking behaviour.

The point does not need to be laboured. The relationship between beliefs, opinions, knowledge and actual *behaviour* is not a straightforward one. What people say in an interview is not the whole picture; adequate research and, in particular, adequate *theorizing*, needs to take account of that.

Index

accuracy 49 50, 91ff
alternatives to interviews 5ff, 12
alternatives to questions 24
analysis grid 64 5
anonymity 15
anxiety/confidence 35
appreciation/understanding 48
audit trail 78

bias 77

case studies 16
Case Study Research Methods 17, 93
category-development 10, 21, 54,
    59ff, 69ff, 73
    subjectivity 70ff
clarification 47
closed questions 41, 66
closure 37, 42ff
confidentiality 8, 15 16
content analysis 9 10, 21, 46, 53
    4, 55 6, 59ff, 73
    procedure 63ff
    practising 66 67
    origins 68

Developing a Questionnaire 13, 21,
    61, 66

development of interview 42,
    53ff, 67

Effective Evaluation 78
élite interviews 21, 81ff
eye contact 31, 33
exemplification 49
extension 49

factual research 17
facial expression 30–1

gesture 31 2
group interviews 21, 87 8
Guba, E.G. and Lincoln, Y.S.
    78
Gutek, B. 92, 93

harrassment 32 3
head nods 31
health/social education 93 4

insight research 17
introduction 37ff

Journal of Social Issues 92
justification 48

length of interviews 12
listening skills 3, 8, 28ff, 51
log-book 19 20

management of interviews 1, 26,
    37ff, 45ff, 54ff
market research 2, 85, 91 2
medical interviews 1, 2, 3, 4
multi-method research 93

narrative construction 74ff
naturalistic research 19, 79
non-directive interviewing 1
non-verbal communication 14,
    30ff, 38ff, 86

observation of self 26ff
open questions 13 14, 41, 45, 66
order of questions 41
organization 37ff, 74

peer review 71 2
personal space 32
physical proximity 32 3
piloting 9, 22, 53ff
posture 33
practising 28 9, 53
presentation 43
prioritizing 54
probes 14, 28, 46ff
prompts 14, 45ff
pruning/selection 20ff

quantitative analysis 76
question development 19ff, 53ff
questioning 51, 53ff
questionnaires 10, 13ff, 19, 20,
    52, 88 9, 92
quotations 76ff

rating scales 92 3
recording 8, 39, 40, 87
recording schedules 14, 21, 88 9
redundancy 60, 61
reflecting 46, 50ff
relevance 48 9
reports 43
representativeness 16, 76
research questions 17
response rate 14
response space 35

sampling 12
satisfaction measures 91ff
schedule 40
self-knowledge 25ff, 91ff
sensitivity of material 15 16, 17
setting 8, 24
silence 35 6
skilled technique 5, 22, 26ff, 39ff
'steering' 36
structure 2, 3ff, 24, 37ff
subjectivity 93
substantive statements 59ff
surveys 16 17, 19

telephone interviews 12, 21, 85ff
therapeutic interviews 2, 3, 16, 42
time-costs 9ff, 18, 62, 85, 89
transcribing 9, 56 7, 61
trialling questions 21ff, 53
trust 16
trustworthiness 78

validity of interview data 93 4
video 25ff, 35, 84 5
voice 34

word-processing 62
writing up 73ff